HELEN SKELTON

Wild GIRL

Illustrated by LIZ KAY

WALKER BOOKS
AND SUBSIDIARIES
LONDON • BOSTON • SYDNEY • AUCKLAND

CONTENTS

ARE YOU READY TO GO WILD?

I grew up on a farm in the middle of nowhere – well, it was
the middle of nowhere to everyone else. To me it was a world full
of limitless adventure. My brother and I and our friends played out later
than we should have, we climbed trees we weren't supposed to and
made up games as we went along. I will be eternally grateful and in
awe of my parents. They taught me to see the fun and opportunity in
every situation, encouraged me to get muddy and told me
never to allow fear to stand in my way.

I've always liked being outdoors more than I liked being indoors, and I've never liked being told I can't  do something. I am no runner, but I've run an ultra-marathon through the Namib Desert. I am no kayaker, but I've kayaked down the Amazon, one of the biggest rivers in the world. I am certainly no high-wire walker and never will be, yet I walked a wire between the towers of Battersea Power Station.

I am very lucky that as a television presenter, I've been a part of some massive adventures in the world's wildest places. I've always been accompanied by an experienced support team and often my adventures have been for charity or to raise awareness about a cause. I know I will never be as accomplished as the adventurers I admire, but they inspire me to think and dream big. I've written this book because I want to share what I've learned: anything is possible if you put your mind to it and try.

Adventures aren't things that happen to other people, they are just your stories in waiting. I want you to get out there and find them. Going wild doesn't have to mean visiting remote or faraway places. You can find adventures everywhere: from your back garden to your local park and at the nearest river or beach. In each chapter, I've given you ideas for different wild or extremely wild adventures and where to find them. There are also stories about real-life wild girls whose amazing feats push me to take on new challenges. I hope they inspire you too.

The most important thing of all is to believe in yourself and be proud of what you achieve. Remember that every challenge is relative and no achievement is more impressive than another. Never let someone tell you that you can't do something, and don't let other people's concerns stop you from trying. Keep moving forwards, embrace the fear, find the positive in every situation and see how far you get. It really doesn't matter if you fail or fall, because as someone once said, you might fly instead.

Have fun, stay safe and unleash your inner wild girl!

Helen Skelton

WELCOME
TO THE
SOUTH POLE

PLEASE FOLLOW THE GROOMED PATH TO
SOUTH POLE STATION ↑

WILD WORLD

Antarctica is the coldest,
windiest and driest continent on
Earth. The coldest temperature
ever recorded was -89°C, and
because the air is so cold, it
never rains.

I love when it snows. My brother and I used to have epic snowball fights that would last for hours, or go sledging on anything we could find. We would stay outside until we were so cold we could hardly feel our toes.

Given how much I loved messing about in the snow, it wasn't really a surprise that I got into skiing. I was lucky enough to go on a school trip and that's when I got the bug for it. Flying down a snowy mountain is a hard feeling to beat. However, I never expected that one day I would travel with a camera crew 500 miles across Antarctica to get to the South Pole, skiing, kite-skiing and cycling across the ice in temperatures of -48°C.

I was taking on the challenge for charity and it was going to be shown on television, so I wanted to push myself to the limit. The aim of my challenge was to be the first person to cycle to the South Pole, which still sounds bonkers. Bikes and snow aren't meant to mix and no one thought that I would be able to cycle through such tough conditions. Yet I believe that if you put your mind to it, anything is possible.

I knew little about Antarctica other than it was at the very bottom of the world. And I knew adventurers, with far more experience than me, had died trying to reach the South Pole. It would take months of planning and training, and the challenge involved a huge support team who were far more experienced in this brutal and dangerous environment than I was. My lungs and limbs needed to be at their best and I was going to have to push my body and my mind to the absolute limit. What I would learn during the experience was humbling – both about myself and this incredible wilderness that we need to preserve and protect.

If I can go from playing in the snow at home to getting all the way to the South Pole, so can you. Follow my journey and then find out how you can have your own adventures in the snow – from your back garden to beyond.

Adventures in ANTARCTICA

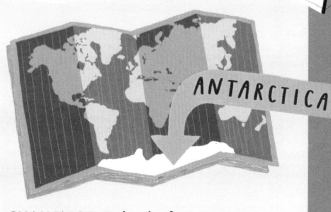

ANTARCTICA

CHALLENGE: To be the first person to use a bike as part of an expedition to the South Pole. As well as travelling on a custom-made bike, I would cover the distance by skiing and kite-skiing.

CROSS-COUNTRY SKI
68 miles

KITE-SKI
329 miles

BIKE
103 miles

DAYS
20 days

JANUARY 5   JANUARY 6   JANUARY 7   JANUARY 8

DISTANCE
500 miles averaging 25 miles per day

  AVERAGE WIND SPEED
80mph

 TEMPERATURE
-48°C

SOUTHERN OCEAN

START
83° SOUTH

FINISH
SOUTH POLE

Geographic
SOUTH POLE

ANTARCTICA

My Trip in NUMBERS

30 nights camping on ice

50 rations of dehydrated food consumed

15 metres of medical tape used on feet

1 wash (with sock and bucket of water)

1 change of underwear

1 Guinness World Record for fastest 100km by kite-ski

500 total miles travelled

TRAINING and PREPARATION

Imagine a cold-weather adventurer. Are you thinking of big men with snowy beards trudging through the ice? Roald Amundsen, Robert Falcon Scott and Ernest Shackleton all survived extreme hardship in their attempts to reach the South Pole (Scott and his men died on the return journey). As I trained for this adventure, I discovered that cold-weather survival is about more than just physical strength. I'm not very tall, I don't have massive muscles and I hope I don't have a beard! But I'm determined, and in that environment mental resilience is important.

I only had six months to prepare, but I was lucky to have three inspirational polar adventurers to show me the ropes. Conrad Dickinson taught me so much about cold-weather survival. Sarah McNair-Landry showed me how to kite-ski. And accompanying me on my adventure was my team-mate, the Norwegian kite-skier and explorer Niklas Norman.

To get used to the extreme cold, I trained in Iceland, New Zealand and Norway. I knew it was going to be impossible to bike the whole distance, so to be confident I had three methods of transport: biking, cross-country skiing and kite-skiing.

As well as being at peak physical fitness, I had to prepare myself mentally. The challenge had so many unknowns. What happened if the bikes didn't work? Or if I got ill? I quickly learned to block out everything other than the training goal in front of me that day.

1 BIKING

I was determined to travel by as much as possible. My custom made bike had wide tyres and thick treads to grip the ice.
Training: I cycled in a wind t to get used to the Antarctic bl I practised riding on the beach because the Antarctic snow is dry it is more like sand than sr I got some strange looks!

2 CROSS-COUNT SKIING

Cross-country skiing is an effic way to cross the ice.
Training: I built up my streng and fitness by running and lift weights. I also tied a tyre arou my waist with rope and dragg it around a field in practice fo pulling the heavy sledge.

3 KITE-SKIING

You can travel at speed an cover huge distances by us a kite to pull your skis. It's exhilarating, but hurts if yo
Training: I had to learn to position and control the kit the wind. I started with a sr training kite before moving full-size one for top speeds

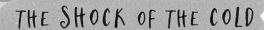

As part of my training, I swallowed an edible thermometer which sent my internal temperature to a computer. I was then tied to a chair and dunked in 10°C water. I stayed in the water until I was so cold, I couldn't spell my own name and was in the early stages of hypothermia. Then I was put in a hot bath to bring my body temperature back up. However, the thermometer showed that my temperature was still falling, despite the fact I felt warmer. It was an important lesson that it was essential to keep my core body temperature above 36°C at all times. I was going to discover that was easier said than done in the freezing cold winds of Antarctica!

KIT LIST

In the cold, your kit is essential to your survival. I learned that the smallest things make a big difference and you have to know your equipment inside out. These are some of the most important things I took with me.

SKI BOOT

Not comfortabl
wear for days

DOWN JACKET

Feels like wearing the warmest duvet ever.

Why take a knife, fork and spoon, if I could take one piece of kit that does all three things?

SPORK

BALACLAVA

It made me look like a bank robber, but it protected my face from the wind, so it was worth it.

FUEL & STOVE

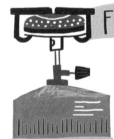

To melt snow for water to drink and to reheat our dried food sachets.

GLOVES

They were the size of oven gloves, because my fingers needed all the protection they could get.

SUNCREAM & SUNGLASSES

The sun is fierce and its glare on white snow can be blinding.

sun cream

60 CHOCOLATE BARS

...mportant as they are high in energy. After ...reaking the bars into individual squares (so ...could eat them in my giant gloves), I was ...otally over chocolate.

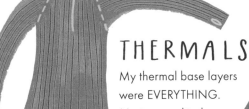

THERMALS

My thermal base layers were EVERYTHING. Merino wool is the best. It kept me toasty and didn't get stinky.

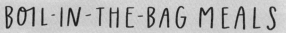

BOIL-IN-THE-BAG MEALS

These freeze-dried sachets are nutritious, easy to use (boil up with melted snow), light to carry and don't go off. Sadly, they aren't very tasty!

SLEDGE

To carry all our equipment. It was very important we didn't take any unnecessary weight, which would slow us down. Still each sledge weighed 82kg, about the weight of a kangaroo.

SMALL SHOVEL

When I had to dig myself out of a drift or create a toilet.

TENT

Home for this adventure!

TENT SLIPPERS

My one luxury item which meant I didn't have to wear boots inside the tent.

PLASTIC SANDWICH BAGS

Essential post-toilet accessories (more on this later).

I had twenty days to cover 500 miles to the South Pole. Everything I needed for that time had to fit inside the small sledge that I would be pulling behind me. The temperature was likely to drop to around -48°C, with winds of up to 80mph. By the time the adventure came around, I was very, very nervous.

FLIGHT TO THE FREEZING WILDS

You can't book a plane ticket and just fly to Antarctica. It is one of the last wildernesses left on Earth. Research scientists live there all year round, but it is still relatively untouched by humans and it takes planning to get there. For the first leg of my journey, I flew from London to Cape Town in South Africa. We then caught a specially arranged flight in an old Russian military plane which had no windows.

   The first challenge was climbing out of the plane in my giant snow boots: imagine a pair of wellies crossed with novelty slippers. All I could see was a vast expanse of white and the wind whipped my breath away. Welcome to Antarctica!

ADAPTING TO ANTARCTICA

I've slept in lots of strange places, and my first night in Antarctica was certainly different. It was almost Christmas Eve and I was thousands of miles away from my friends and family.

TOILET TRAINING

There is nowhere to hide in Antarctica. It is wall-to-wall white, and there are no bushes or rocks to run behind. So when you need the loo, you just have to go. Mortifying to begin with, but at least doing a poo shows your body is healthy and working normally, something by the end of an expedition you care far more about than any embarrassed faces. In Antarctica, it's too cold for bugs to survive, so there's nothing to break down human waste. It just freezes on the snow. That's why anything you "do" (both number ones and number twos), has to go into a sandwich bag or plastic bottle. Then you seal it up and take it off the ice with you when you leave. I recommend practising your aim into a sandwich bag. And you mustn't muddle the bag with your chocolate ration!

It also never got dark, which made it difficult to sleep. Because of the way the Earth tilts towards the sun, in Antarctica there are 24 hours of daylight in the summer and 24 hours of darkness in the winter. I was there in January, which in the Southern Hemisphere makes it the summer. Because of the constant daylight, I kept waking up.

There were lots of things I was going to have to adapt to and luckily I had a few days before the training leg began to get to grips with the environment. Home for the next six weeks was going to be a tent, so one of the first things to practise was putting up a tent quickly. It was important that Niklas and I were confident that if a storm came we could make shelter quickly. Tents are a bit of a faff at the best of times, but try assembling one while wearing mittens that look like oven gloves. It took me a few attempts before I was able to do it quickly.

The other thing to adjust to was the cold. The top priority in Antarctica is to stay warm, and that meant trapping heat by wearing lots of layers rather than one thick jumper. During the first few days as we tried out the kit, I learned that the big advantage of layers is that you can take something off if you get hot and then put it back on when you get cold. It was essential though to keep my hands, feet and face covered at all times. You only want to expose your bare flesh to the elements if you really have to – such as when you need to go to the loo.

The TRAINING LEG

Before our official challenge began, we had ten days to test our kit in the real conditions. At this point we had only tested the bikes on sand, so we needed to find out if they were going to work on ice. And I still needed to build my confidence with the kite.

The original training plan was to travel about 12 miles a day and set up camp each evening, but a massive snowstorm struck. With winds of 70mph and lots of fresh snow, we had no choice but to wait it out in our tents for two days. The snow was so heavy the tents were collapsing under the weight. We took it in turns to dig the tents out to stop them ripping. Standing outside the shelter of the tent, the wind was so strong, it was impossible for me to stand upright. I realized then how dangerous Antarctica could be, which was both terrifying and strangely exciting.

SKIING SHAMBLES

When the storm cleared, it was time to start training with cross-country skis. Niklas and I were each pulling a heavy sledge with our food, tent and equipment, often uphill. This was the first time I had spent 10 hours in my ski boots and my feet got blisters almost immediately. I didn't want to stop and cause a fuss, especially as we'd already lost two days, so I stayed silent. By the end of the first day I had a blister the size of a fifty pence piece on my left foot, which was agony when it rubbed against the hard plastic boot. I should have got the blister treated by the medical team, and my feet were in pain for the rest of the adventure.

Practising with the kite was far more fun. Niklas could ski close enough to give me tips on mastering the big, powerful kite. I had a couple of nasty falls on the hard ice, but I loved the feeling of travelling at speed. The landscape was epic too: bright blue sky and white untouched snow.

DANGER ZONE! BLISTERS

Blisters aren't dangerous. WRONG. I've met adventurers who have had to end trips because of blisters. Avoidable, annoying blisters. The key is prevention. Make sure your boots fit and your socks are clean. If you start to feel rubbing or pain, stop immediately, put on a blister plaster and adjust your socks and boots to relieve the pressure on the area.

BIKE TEST

One of the things I was most excited about was being the first person to use a bike to get to the South Pole. Everyone had said it was impossible and it was the part of the challenge I hadn't really been able to train for, because the snow in Antarctica is so different from snow anywhere else in the world. As it never rains, the snow isn't wet and fluffy. It is grainy and hard, more like sand. Niklas was worried the bikes wouldn't cope in the conditions and the first time we tried them, with the sledges attached, we only covered 1.5 miles in about an hour and a half. Even without the sledges it was unbelievably hard work and my thighs ached from pedalling. The challenge was to use the bikes for as much of the 500 miles as possible, and I was beginning to see how difficult that was going to be.

HAPPY NEW YEAR

We finished the training leg on New Year's Day. I washed and changed my clothes for the first time in ten days. I was happy we now had a daily routine: wake up, wee in a bottle, melt snow for water, eat a boil-in-the-bag meal, take down the tent, move for up to 10 hours, then fight the exhaustion to make camp again. I was still nervous though, because training had shown that the bikes were the weakness in our plan.

JOURNEY to the SOUTH POLE

On the first official day of the challenge, we set off at a longitude of 83° south at 2,200 metres above sea level. To make the 500-mile distance to the South Pole in twenty days, we had to cover a minimum of 25 miles a day using the bikes, skis or the kites. The pressure was on.

I knew Niklas was worried that the bikes would use up a huge amount of our energy without covering enough distance. Travelling to the South Pole on bikes was the whole point of the challenge, so I was determined to use them. It was exhausting. The ice parted like sand under our tyres and moving a few metres felt like running a marathon. Any dip or bump meant grinding to a halt. On our first day, with some cycling and quite a lot of pushing, we only managed 15 miles, well short of our 25-mile target. That night at camp, we didn't really talk to each other. We should have been working as a team, so this wasn't the best start.

On the second day, we woke up to a strong wind. It was perfect for kite-skiing and we covered a whopping 41 miles. We decided that by making the most of the windy weather by kite-skiing, we could make up for the slow-going bikes. If it was too hard-going on the bikes, or visibility was poor, we would cross-country ski. We began to make good progress each day. Even Niklas admitted that when there wasn't much wind, the bikes weren't a bad way to travel. At the half-way point, it was a relief to see that we had covered many more miles by bike than anyone would have expected at the start.

KITES AWAY

Kite-skiing became my favourite way to travel. Although the snow looks flat, the wind carves it into sharp, wave-like ridges and you have to move around them. You can still go fast: my fastest speed was 15mph. We decided it would be fun to try for a World Record: the fastest kite-skiing speed over 100km (about 62 miles). Even though many

DANGER ZONE! CREVASSES

Ice isn't smooth or flat. Thick sheets of ice are called glaciers and there can be cracks in them, known as crevasses, that are hundreds of metres deep. You have to keep your eyes constantly on the snow ahead of you. If in doubt, poke the snow before you stand on it to check if it is solid.

kite-skiers have travelled further or faster, no one had set a record for specifically 100km. I did it in 7 hours and 28 minutes.

DEHYDRATION DRAMA

During the long days on the ice, I didn't want to have to stop, take off my gloves and unscrew my water bottle every time I needed a drink. One evening, the medical team tested my urine. It was dark orange, which meant I was dehydrated. It explained my constant headache – it wasn't from the lack of oxygen in the air because of the altitude, but because my body desperately needed water. I drunk lots of water to rehydrate. Only once my wee was straw-coloured, could I safely carry on.

When we were about a week from the Pole, I made the decision to stop using the kites and cover the rest of the distance on the bikes and skis. Niklas thought this was a bad idea, but I was determined to use the bikes as much as possible, even though it would be agony.

Our pace immediately fell through the floor from around 40 miles a day to 20 miles. When the snow was soft, we had no option but to get off and push the bikes or switch to cross-country skiing. We were using more energy, so we were stopping often to eat and drink. We snacked on a mixture of nuts, chocolate, sweets, cheese and dried meat. It was all mixed up in the same bag so it was a lucky dip. When you're that hungry, you don't care.

It was much harder to stay warm when we were moving so slowly. The other danger was getting wet – not from rain or snow, but from sweat. In Antarctica, if you get wet, you can catch hypothermia and die. Unlike anywhere else in the world, you can't take off your hood or peel back your balaclava to cool down because that exposes your extremities to frostbite. Towards the end, my biggest fear was getting ill and being unable to complete the challenge.

DANGER ZONE! FROSTBITE

When you're exposed to the cold, your body tries to stay warm by increasing the blood flow to your main organs, such as your heart and lungs. The blood flow in the extremities of your body – your fingers and toes – slows down. In severe cases, the lack of blood flow can lead to frostbite, which is when the flesh turns black and starts to die. Frostbite has caused many adventurers to lose fingers and toes. The British explorer, Sir Ranulph Fiennes, cut off his own black frostbitten fingers with a saw (which he showed me). You can avoid frostbite by wearing the right kit and keeping your skin covered. Pins and needles or redness are bad signs. Always make sure you can feel your fingers and toes.

LOW POINT

In the final few days we were on the move for 14 hours a day. One day, with about 100 miles to go, I felt totally overwhelmed and I cried. I immediately regretted it because I knew how lucky I was to be skiing (and cycling) in the footsteps of some of the world's greatest adventurers. However, I was physically and mentally drained.

Every muscle ached. I wanted to be with my family at home, warm and dry. But deep down I knew I couldn't be this close and give up now. All I had to do was focus on how far I had come and believe that I could keep going just a tiny bit further. My mind had to become stronger than my legs. I could do it. I could get there.

FINAL COUNTDOWN

With two days to go, I was battling a bad cough and the almost unbearable wind chill. It wasn't until we hit 89° south (about 60 miles from the South Pole), that I began to imagine we would make it.

On the final day we decided to kite-ski. It was bliss. The cloudless sky meant the ice sparkled. We covered the distance at speed and I felt amazing. A few months ago, the kites had terrified me and here I was about to make it. I punched the air and underneath my balaclava my face ached from smiling.

As the South Pole Station became more than a dot on the horizon, every single part of my body hurt but I didn't care. We cycled the final hundred metres, trying to hold hands as we pedalled. It had been such a team effort: without Niklas and his masterminding of kit and logistics we never would have made it. Together, we entered the circle of flags and I put my hands on the globe marking the South Pole. This was it. The bottom of the world.

21

Adventure REPORT

Reaching the finish line was such a mix of feelings: happiness, pride and relief that we'd made it. I was also sad the adventure was over. The environment was tough, but I enjoyed working so hard each day. There was great satisfaction in chalking up the miles and closing in on a target that seemed impossible at the beginning.

Would I have done anything differently? In the early stages, I'd been so determined to churn out the miles, I wish I'd taken the experience in more. I guess that's why people tell you not to worry about what is in front or behind you, and just take each day as it comes.

Memories of the stark Antarctic landscape will stay with me for ever. I was so lucky to have explored one of the world's last wildernesses. The South Pole is a precious place and I certainly came back thinking how important it is we protect it in whatever ways we can.

BEST BITS

1 Cycling the final few metres to the South Pole with Niklas. Words cannot describe the feeling.

Spending Christmas Day and New Year's Day in such a remote otherworldly landscape. It was a once in a lifetime experience.

3 Kite-skiing at speed. Whipping along the Antarctic snow underneath an epic kite made me feel pretty cool.

WORST BITS

1 The day with -41°C wind chill. It felt like a knife was scraping down my face.

2 Getting diarrhoea while living in a tent with nowhere to wash. That was a challenge.

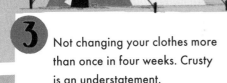

3 Not changing your clothes more than once in four weeks. Crusty is an understatement.

HORRIBLE HAIR

At the end of the training leg, my hair looked like a matted rat's tail. The crew let me wash it in some soap and water. The issue was drying it. It's so cold in Antarctica you can't walk around with soaking wet hair. It could kill you. So they altered the settings on a blowtorch, and as soon as I had washed my hair, I used the torch to dry it (DON'T TRY THIS AT HOME). Coming back, I've never been so happy to use my hairdryer again.

OH FOR AN APPLE

The first thing I ate when I came off the ice was an apple. I had gone weeks eating dehydrated fruit and boil-in-the-bag meals that tasted like sawdust and I longed for something fresh. I have never taken fruit for granted since.

WILD ADVENTURES

Not everyone can or should go to the South Pole. You can, however, have heaps of fun with your family and friends in the snow closer to home.

1 Sledging

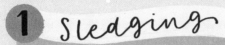

You don't need a lot of snow or a sledge. A strong plastic bag, tray, dog bed, yoga mat or air mattress are options you might find around the house. Check with your dog first. A hill is good, but if your garden or closest park is flat you could always just get a friend or family member to drag you along.

WARNING
Adult supervision required for adventures.

2 Snowball FIGHTS

The simplest fun anyone can have in the snow. Keep a spare pair of gloves in your pocket, so when your fingers get wet and cold from the snow you can swap to your second pair. Plastic bags inside your wellies will keep your feet warm and dry too.

3 ICE Skating

A fun way to experience ice for the first time. Lots of towns and cities have ice-skating rinks. Don't forget to wear clothes that are easy to move in and cover your body. Also take gloves and warm socks.

COLD FINGERS? WALK LIKE A PENGUIN

If my fingers are cold, I lock my arms down by my side and bend my wrists at right angles away from my body. Then I pump my shoulders up and down as fast as I can. This sends blood to the ends of your fingertips and warms them up.

4 SKIING

Skiing is an incredible and exhilarating way to experience the snow. I love downhill skiing, which is when you use the momentum of the mountain to swish down the hill. Cross-country skiing, when you propel yourself across the snow, is harder work as it is all down to you, but is a great way to explore a snowy landscape at a slower pace.

5 Snowboarding

Snowboarding is wicked. Instead of moving down the mountain on two skis, your feet are strapped to a board. The boots are comfier than ski boots, but knee pads are also a good idea, as it can be harder to balance and stop.

6 KITE-Skiing

Before trying kite-skiing it helps to be a confident skier, snowboarder or skateboarder, but if you get the chance to try it, it is epic. You are harnessed to a kite and the most important thing is to align your feet and the kite, or the wind will whip you off your feet. When you get it right, it's an unbelievable feeling: you go fast, you feel cool and it's not tiring. In fact, it's easier than surfing or kite-surfing in the sea, because you start standing up.

WHERE to go WILD

Your local indoor ski slope
Get a taste for skiing at your nearest indoor dry slope or snow dome. You can have lessons to help you master the basics before you go out on the snow.

Scotland
The Scottish ski resorts: Glenshee and the Cairngorms are my faves. Both have Disability Snowsport UK groups.

French Alps
There are incredible views and glaciers for world-class skiing and snowboarding. I like the variety of the slopes at Val Thorens: there's everything from gentle to nail-biting.

Finse, Norway
A favourite training ground for the world's most accomplished adventurers.

EXTREMELY WILD ADVENTURES

Extremely wild cold adventures will take planning and training. Think about getting support from a professional adventurer or a trained guide.

1 WALK ACROSS A GLACIER

Glaciers are vast sheets of frozen ice formed on mountains over thousands of years. Crossing a glacier on foot, using poles and shoes fitted with crampons to give you grip, is an incredible experience that will reward you with stunning views. Watch out for crevasses!

2 ICE CLIMBING

Ice climbing requires concentration, strength and strategy. Using ice axes, crampons and ropes, you can climb up walls of ice or frozen waterfalls. Dangers include frostbite, avalanches and falling to your death. Start out on an indoor wall to learn the basics and enjoy the adrenaline rush when you get to the top.

WARNING
Adult supervision required for adventures.

3 SLEEP in a SNOW HOLE

This is a great survival skill to learn in case your tent rips or you find yourself caught out in bad weather. Don't get wet when you dig the hole or you will quickly get cold. I slept in a snow hole in New Zealand when training for Antarctica and it was a cold, dark and lonely experience. Building a snow hole can be dangerous, so make sure you are with an expert and following professional advice. Leave a marker on the surface so people can find you.

INSIDE the ICE
— Helen's Report —

In Alaska, I tried ice climbing out of a moulin, a hole where water enters a glacier. They are so dangerous even my experienced guide was scared. Moulins are very deep and if you fall into one there is no way out. When I lowered myself over the edge, I was so terrified I couldn't breathe.

As I used the ropes to inch my way down the wall of ice, the thundering waterfall beside me was deafening. I kept going until I was past the water and I found a ledge to rest on. Being inside the glacier felt like being inside a diamond. The sunlight from the surface bounced off every angle, crack and crease, creating beams of light like lasers. I took it in, then began to climb to the top.

With an ice axe in each hand, I was able to grip the wall and inch my way back to the top. Even though the crampons and axes are sharp, they barely pierce the ice, so I had to trust that the small spikes would take my body weight. I moved slowly. Deliberately. It took me so long that the muscles in my arms and legs were burning. I reached the top exhausted and elated. I have never been so relieved to be on cold, hard ice again.

WHERE to go WILD

The Ice Factor National Ice Climbing Centre, Scotland
One of the biggest ice walls in the world, where you can learn the ropes.

Kenai Fjords National Park, USA
Enjoy the epic glaciers and vast fjords, and eat s'mores by a campfire.

Wanaka, New Zealand
I learned to kite-ski on untouched pistes – it felt off the beaten track.

Vatnajökull, Iceland
Magical landscapes at every turn, and a chance to see the largest glacier in Europe.

WILD GIRL TOP TIP

For any adventure in the extreme cold, it is essential you know how to cope with all eventualities. A cold-weather survival course is a great way to learn vital skills such as making shelter and finding food and water.

WILD GIRL Wall of Fame

Be inspired by these incredible women's cold adventures.

Felicity Aston

Felicity Aston is the first woman to ski across Antarctica alone, covering 1,034 miles in 59 days. She pulled two sledges with 85kg of food and equipment, and is the first person to cross Antarctica using muscle power only, with no help from kites or machines.

BARBARA HILLARY

Barbara Hillary became the first African-American woman to reach the North Pole in 2007. She was 75 years old! She loved her adventure so much that four years later she reached the South Pole too, making her both the first African-American woman and one of the oldest people to reach both poles.

Barbara 2007

Jackie Ronne

In 1947, aged 28, Jackie Ronne became the first woman to explore Antarctica as a working member of an expedition. She stayed in the freezing temperatures of Antarctica for over a year, making scientific observations and writing news releases and daily reports on the expedition. The Ronne Ice Shelf in Antarctica is named after her.

ANN BANCROFT & LIV ARNESEN

Ann Bancroft and Liv Arnesen became the first women to complete a transcontinental crossing of Antarctica. Inspired by Sir Ernest Shackleton, they travelled 1,717 miles in 94 days, sailing and skiing while pulling heavy sledges through the -34°C chills and 100mph winds.

Ann + Liv 2001

20ᵗʰ JAN 2018

THE ICE MAIDENS
Six soldiers in the British Army

Six soldiers in the British Army and polar novices became the first all-female team to cross Antarctica using muscle power alone. They completed the 1,056-mile trek, pulling sledges full of supplies and equipment and skiing for over 10 hours a day, in just 62 days – well ahead of their 75-day target. They broke four World Records!

Sarah McNair-Landry is the youngest person to travel to both the South and North Poles, at 18 and 19 respectively. She is an accomplished kite-skier and dog-team handler and is recognized as a Master Polar Guide.

Sarah McNair-Landry

INSERT PHOTO HERE

YOU!

WHERE WILL YOUR NEXT ADVENTURE TAKE YOU?

ADVENTURES

WILD WORLD

The Namib Desert is one of the world's oldest deserts, at least 55 million years old. Temperatures can reach as high as 50°C during the day and drop below 0°C at night. Some areas receive less than 10mm of rain each year.

n the SAND

Although I've always loved being outdoors, at school I wouldn't have said I was naturally sporty. I definitely wasn't one of the girls who did cross-country. When I first heard about a marathon, I remember thinking that the idea of running 26 miles in one go was crazy. How could that be fun? Yet something about long-distance running, especially in extreme conditions, fascinated me.

For years I had followed the Marathon des Sables, a six-day ultra-marathon event in the Sahara Desert. With no shade or shelter, the runners covered a total distance of around 155 miles in temperatures of 50°C and with limited water. The conditions were brutal. I was so impressed with the way that the runners pushed themselves to the limit yet managed to cross the finish line smiling. So when the opportunity came up to take on a big challenge for a television programme, I immediately thought of an ultra-marathon in the desert.

My friend discovered a new race in Namibia, which is in southwest Africa. Like the Marathon des Sables, it was a desert ultra-marathon, but the challenge was to run three marathons (78 miles in total) in 24 hours. I jumped at the chance, rather impulsively given my only previous experience was that I had once run a half-marathon for fun. That was 13 miles, and I wasn't fast and I didn't find it easy. I knew I was taking on a real challenge, where every step would be filmed, and I don't think anyone seriously thought I could run 78 miles in temperatures of up to 42°C. No one. Not even my parents, who are the most supportive people in the world.

I only had three months to train so running became my life. To start with, I wanted to prove the people who doubted me wrong, but I quickly learned not to worry about what other people had to say. Instead I needed to focus on what I could achieve in such an extreme environment. When you do that, the possibilities for adventure are as endless as grains of sand in the desert.

Adventures in NAMIBIA

CHALLENGE: To complete three marathons within 24 hours, I was going to have to run through the heat of the day and through the night.

MEANS OF TRANSPORT
Foot

DISTANCE
78 miles

CHECKPOINTS
6

TIME LIMIT
24 hours

TEMPERATURE
Highs of 42°C, lows of 0°C

N A M I B

SOUTH ATLANTIC OCEAN

FINISI

AFRICA

NAMIBIA

START

My Trip in NUMBERS

3
months of preparation

747
miles clocked up training

23
competitors in the race

23
hours and 50 minutes
finishing time

FINISH

8TH
place finish

2ND
woman to
complete
course

TRAINING and PREPARATION

I have never thought of myself as a natural runner. I still don't find running easy, but what I do enjoy is thinking something is impossible and then proving to myself that I can do it. There were three women running in my ultra-marathon. My training taught me that a huge part of endurance running is mental strength. My challenge was going to be staying in the race and not giving up.

My first run was outside my parents' house. I jogged for all of 10 minutes and I swear I nearly collapsed. I had signed up for the race by that point though, and I didn't want to pull out because I knew if I quit this, I could quit anything. So I kept running for 10 minutes until I could tackle 20 minutes, then 30. I still remember the feeling the first time I ran for an hour on a treadmill. That's when I knew I could probably do the ultra-marathon if I just got on with it instead of worrying about it.

Because I only had three months to prepare, I was running almost every day. I actually think having such a short training period was a good thing. If I'd had a year, I would have got bored or injured and found excuses not to train, thinking there was plenty of time. With such a short time frame, I had to make every day count. I ran everywhere with a little backpack containing a change of clothes. As the saying goes, I was training hard to race easy, putting in the miles so I could run with confidence in Namibia.

Running rewards your body quickly. That motivated me. I became addicted to seeing my progress. I was also lucky that I had a fantastic trainer. Rory Coleman has run over a thousand marathons and he coaxed me through tears and tantrums

The Marathon des Sables is a six-day ultra-marathon event in which participants run the equivalent of six marathons across the brutal Sahara Desert in Morocco, Africa. You have to carry everything you need with you and water is rationed. My Namibia experience was partly inspired by the British adventurer Ben Fogle, who signed up to do the Marathon des Sables when he had never run a marathon before and had only six weeks to train. If he could take on one of the hardest endurance races in the world and finish it, why couldn't I try something similar?

when my legs hurt so much I didn't think I could run another pace. I went to bed each night in agony and woke up stiff. I was determined to gain experience in as many challenging conditions as possible. I signed up for a 10km, a 13km and a 20km, then finally ran my first marathon.

I felt intimidated turning up to events where everyone else would be wearing high-tech kit, doing stretches I had never seen before and talking about their race strategies. I had to learn the hard way to block all of that out. It didn't matter what other people did. I just had to focus on what I was capable of achieving. Music helped hugely. I had a playlist of songs that spurred me on through my training.

MARATHON PRACTICE SESSIONS

1 London

Rory persuaded me to run a marathon through London. We followed the route of the Circle Line on the Underground but through the streets. I clocked up 26 miles at a snail's pace. It took me about 8 hours. That's ridiculously slow in running circles, but the point was I'd done my first marathon.

2 Cumbria

I ran from the Cumbrian coast to the bottom of Scafell Pike through snow, ice and torrential rain, completing two marathons on two consecutive days to get my mileage up. My trousers were so heavy with water that I had to stop every few metres to hitch them up. It was a good lesson in the importance of the right kit.

3 Morocco

I went to Morocco to get a feel for what it would be like to run in the desert. I didn't really have a route, just a dirt track to follow and things quickly went wrong. I did manage to practise cooking at a made-up checkpoint and going to the toilet. The heat was so draining and exhausting that I quickly broke down, overwhelmed by the challenge facing me.

KIT LIST

I had to carry everything I needed to survive in the extreme heat for 24 hours, including food, water and first aid. Any excess weight would slow me down so I had to carefully consider what to pack in my rucksack.

RUCKSACK

As I was going to be carrying it for 24 hours, it needed to be as small, light and comfortable as possible.

TRAINERS

I had trail-running trainers with thick soles to cushion my feet from the rocky ground.

LONG SLEEVE SHIRT & LEGGINGS

I needed to cover as much of my skin from the sun as possible. I stupidly wore knee-length leggings and my legs were so sunburnt, I was in agony.

SUNGLASSES

The glare of the sun was blinding. I needed sunglasses that didn't move as I ran and didn't let light in around the sides.

CAP

Essential to protect my head and face from the heat of the sun.

SUNCREAM

Absolutely essential for the strong sun. More is better.

WATER

I carried my water on my back in a special pouch with a long hose to drink from so I could keep sipping water without having to stop and get my bottle out of my rucksack.

COMFORTABLE SPORTS UNDERWEAR

Never wear anything next to your skin that could rub or chafe. I learned this the hard way.

BLISTER PADS & TAPE

My feet were probably the most important piece of kit I had, so it was important I looked after them. I cut the tape into strips before I set off to save time in the race itself.

NUTS & SPORTS GELS

They're high in protein and energy as well as being light and easy to carry. Some people also took boil-in-the-bag meals and a stove so they could eat at the checkpoints.

HEAD TORCH

My only light as I ran through the darkness in the middle of the night.

FIRST-AID KIT & SPACE BLANKET

Ultra-marathon events can be spread out and result in long gaps between the runners. It could take a while to be rescued, so I needed to be prepared.

TOILET ROLL

Running makes you need a poo – I got used to doing wild wees and poos!

I had a single day to cover three marathons (78 miles) across the Namib Desert. I would be running through the glare of the midday sun and the total darkness of the night. Although I had trained intensively for three months, I didn't have much experience of running in temperatures of 42°C. By the time the race came around, I was ready to take on the challenge, but scared of what lay ahead.

PRE-RACE NERVES

We spent a few days before the race camping near the start line. It was a great way to meet the other competitors. Twenty-three people had signed up. To say I stuck out was an understatement. Everyone else was dressed in running kit, and I turned up wearing a polka-dot dress and flip-flops. Of course I was intimidated. The other competitors had all taken part in dozens of events and clocked up thousands of miles between them. Some of them had even run this race before and there was talk about people being hospitalized after last year.

DANGER ZONE! HEATSTROKE

Heatstroke happens when the body overheats and can't cool down. It normally happens after spending too long in the sun or doing too much exercise in high temperatures. Symptoms include headaches, sickness and dizziness. If it isn't treated quickly it can damage your vital organs and, in extreme cases, lead to death.

I asked one of the previous competitors what it was like. "Like running into a wall of fire," he replied. There's not a lot you can say to that. I found it difficult not to get sucked in to what everyone around me was saying and let it affect my confidence.

SAFETY CHECKS

The day before the race, the event organizers checked through all our kit to make sure we were carrying the necessary safety equipment and briefed us on the dangers of running through a desert, which included being bitten by snakes. In the heat, we were going to sweat so we were at risk from dehydration and

WILD WORLD
SNAKES

There are over 70 species of snake in Namibia. We were briefed to watch our feet in the knee-length grass: "Avoid being at the back of the pack. You are more likely to get bitten if you are at the back. The first runners will wake them up and those at the back will be prime targets." Not exactly the motivation I wanted, but it did make me hurdle a few questionable clumps of grass. Other dangers were spiders and hyenas.

heatstroke. We were told the signs to watch out for. The organizers also told us if we couldn't keep up with the pace at any point, we would be pulled off the course.

ON THE START LINE

Despite my nerves, I slept well in my tent that night and woke up in a really good mood. The moment I had trained so hard for was finally here.

The early morning sun was low but it still made everything glow a bright orange. We were due to set off at 9.00 a.m. and on the start line, everyone was on edge. It was that sort of nervous excitement where no one quite knew what was going to happen next. When the starting hooter sounded, I actually squealed with excitement. I could finally start chalking off the miles. Whatever the race threw at me, this was going to be an unforgettable experience.

The FIRST MARATHON
(0-26 MILES)

I always knew that running across a desert was going to be hard. However, it wasn't until the first marathon that I realized just how intense the challenge was going to be. The first marathon was through the hottest part of the day. They were the hardest 26 miles I've ever run. My race almost ended before it began.

Once the hooter sounded, I set off quickly, because I didn't want to be at the back and a target for the snakes. Going too fast too soon was a terrible idea. The temperature climbed to 42°C and there was no shelter from the glare of the sun. I had applied suncream, but my exposed legs were still burning. In the intense heat, I quickly became drained of energy. I forced myself to slow to a walk. The first checkpoint was at 13 miles, and even before then the medical staff had pulled two people off the course because they were suffering from heat-related illnesses.

I kept putting one foot in front of the other, thinking of the second checkpoint. I was exhausted, I hadn't eaten enough and I was starting to panic. I had yet to complete a marathon, but already I was floundering.

In the heat, I became dehydrated and started to hallucinate. I thought I could see wind turbines on the horizon. The pack of runners had spread out and I was alone. The ankle-deep sand was sapping my energy. Overwhelmed, I crouched in the shade of a bush, trying to cool myself down. I drank water and

DANGER ZONE! DEHYDRATION

Dehydration happens when your body loses more fluid than it takes in. When it's hot and you're doing extreme exercise, you sweat lots so it's important to drink lots of water and fluids to replace the water you're losing. Feeling dizzy and lightheaded, headaches, tiredness and very dark, strong-smelling urine (or not weeing at all) are all signs that your body needs more water quickly.

WILD WORLD: THE NAMIB DESERT

The desert was vast and never-ending. I have never experienced heat like it. The parched ground was so hot it was radiating heat. There was no escape. Sometimes the ground glowed orange, sometimes it was sandy and sometimes it was rocky. It's inhospitable, but home to some of Africa's most striking wildlife, including the endangered black rhino, the hyena, the oryx, the ostrich and even elephants. I would have loved to have seen these animals during the race, but it was probably for the best I didn't! The closest we got were some elephant tracks.

even though I felt sick and dizzy, I ate some nuts for energy. In the heat eating was the last thing I wanted to do, but I knew without the calories, my race would be over.

FINDING A FRIEND

One of the other runners, Fran, caught up with me. He had started the race at a walking pace, and as a result wasn't suffering quite so much from the heat. He got me back on my feet and I walked at his pace beside him and we started to chat. Fran's positive outlook was exactly the distraction I needed. Without that bit of camaraderie and teamwork, I think my race would have ended behind that bush.

Fran and I kept walking and talking. The landscape was epic. It was what I imagine another planet would look like, with huge craters and rocky cracks in the ground. I tried not to think about how much my feet hurt. You know when you stub your toe and the pain shoots through your body? It felt like that every time I put one foot on the ground. There was pain in every stride.

After 9 hours and the second checkpoint, I had clocked one marathon. It had been so much harder than I had ever anticipated.

The SECOND MARATHON (26 - 52 MILES)

I reached the checkpoint at the end of the first marathon feeling broken. There were a dozen people slumped on the ground. Some were shivering. Some were eating. Some were taping up their blisters. Few were talking. I felt like I had walked into a scene from a disaster movie. It was clear that everyone was struggling. As awful as it sounds, it actually made me feel a bit better. At least it wasn't just me who was finding the race hard.

I sat down, unsure if I would be able to get back up again, and forced myself to eat one of the boil-in-the-bag meals I had in my rucksack. They taste disgusting, but by this stage I really needed energy from a proper meal. I peeled back my socks to reveal massive blisters. I taped them up with pads, trying to ignore the intense pain. I discovered that a total of five people had pulled out and only eighteen of us were left.

   It was now 6.00 p.m. We did the calculations and if I carried on at my current pace, I would never finish within 24 hours. Someone told me I should just enjoy the view as it was so unlikely I would finish. Determined to prove them wrong, I got on my feet, ready to shuffle off into the night.

NIGHT IN THE DESERT

The burnt orange sand had been swallowed by
endless darkness. Finally the temperature dropped.
Ten hours of darkness and two more marathons
awaited me. There was no getting away from the
exhaustion, the pain and the fact that I was towards
the back of the field.

The small white light from my head torch was the
only way I could see where I was going. Every time
I moved my feet I could hear creatures scuttling. All
I could do was look for the glow-stick route markers
and keep plodding on. The stars spread out in the sky
above me. One by one the head torches that were behind me disappeared
as people dropped out. Time was snapping at my heels and I felt very alone.
Then the support truck drove past me with Fran in the back. His feet were too
blistered for him to carry on. The steward asked me how much longer I'd last.
I didn't know, but I knew I had to keep trying.

PUSHING THROUGH THE PAIN

Soon my socks were stuck to my feet with sweat and pus. I was trying to pad
my blisters again when the last of the stewards drove up to me. "You got
further than we thought!" he said. That was the comment I needed to kick me
up the bottom. It was time to stop wallowing and get on with it. I had been in
pain for weeks training, so what was a few more hours of agony?

I started walking. At one point I shouted "I cannot quit!" over and over.
Then I made myself run three paces at a time until the balance of pain had
shifted, and it was harder to stop than run.

By 2.00 a.m. my blisters were so big the race doctor had to pop them with
a scalpel to drain out the pus. I considered pulling out. Then I thought about
telling people I had failed, and that hurt more than my feet. I began to run,
telling myself that each mile was one I never had to do again. Eventually I
saw the checkpoint for the end of the second marathon.

The THIRD MARATHON
(52 - 78 MILES)

At 3.22 a.m. having completed 52 miles, two thirds of the race, I lay on my hands and knees at the checkpoint. I was alone apart from the medical staff. Everyone else had come and gone. I had been awake for 21 hours, and in the race for 18 hours. If I was to stand any chance of finishing this challenge, I would have to run my final marathon quicker than any marathon I had ever done in training.

I stopped at the checkpoint for less than 5 minutes. I set off screaming, unable to contain my agony. Only now I did not want to stop. "Come on me!" I shouted into the night. It was the only thing I could do to drown out the pain. I was running though. Against the odds, I was still running.

At the final checkpoint before the finish, there were others resting. I cannot explain what a glorious feeling it was to see other people after 7 hours alone, in pain and in the dark. Yet even though I was elated to see them, I didn't have any time to chat. The final 13 miles were now a race against the clock. I had spent months in the gym, hours running on my own, and it all came down to now. This was the race. This was where I had to dig deep. I had only half a marathon to go and I knew I could do that. I just had to get going.

SUNRISE FINISH

It was still chilly but the sun was beginning to creep over the horizon. The thought of having to run through the heat of the day again terrified me. The sooner I finished the sooner I would be safe from the fiery ball in the sky. At 6.17 a.m., with the sun starting to throw out its light, I hit the tarmac road that I knew led to the finish line. The final few miles were agony as my legs seized up, but I was so close that quitting was not an option. The last mile was the hardest thing I have ever done. I crossed the finish line at 8.50 a.m., 23 hours and 50 minutes into the race. I was within 10 minutes of the 24-hour time limit.

21

FINISH

Adventure REPORT

1

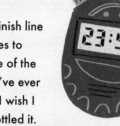

Crossing the finish line with 10 minutes to spare was one of the best feelings I've ever experienced. I wish I could have bottled it.

I went into the ultra-marathon trying to prove people wrong. But the experience quickly taught me not to let other people's opinions knock my confidence. The race showed me that sometimes you just have to keep your head down and plough on, using the highs to get you through the lows.

WORST BITS

1 Having to run in such intense and draining heat. I was lucky to finish – the temperature made many of the runners too ill to complete the course.

I will be eternally grateful to my fellow competitors. Without people like Fran and the amazing team spirit, I would never have got through the race. They taught me the importance of staying positive. Now I know there will always be a low point in a big event, but it is important to be able to embrace that feeling and know that around the next corner you will feel better. All you can do is take the tough bits a few paces at a time.

BRA BLISTERS

I also learned to test my kit. I ran a training race in an underwired sports bra and the wire pierced the skin on my chest. By the time I got home, my bra was stuck to my chest with blood and I had to sit in the bath to soak my top off.

46

2

Namibia is one of the most stunning places I have ever been lucky enough to visit. It's like being on another planet. The orange desert, the craggy ancient rocks and the rugged coastline are unbelievably beautiful.

3

The incredible team spirit made the race for me. I have so much love and respect for the people who signed up for that race. I wouldn't have finished were it not for them. I am in awe of those runners and grateful for their support and motivation.

3

I'm glad I trained as hard as I did, but some of my training runs made me want to give up before I'd even run the race. I don't miss the aches, pains and having to run in all weathers, no matter what.

2

My giant, painful pus-filled blisters. After 24 hours of running, I had blisters so big I couldn't keep my trainers on.

TOENAIL TRAUMA

It is beyond gross but I carried all ten of my toenails around in my purse for weeks after the ultra-marathon. Running had made my nails so fragile they just pinged off my toes. It didn't hurt, but it looked awful. I was quite proud of what I had been through, so I used to freak people out by asking them if they could guess what I was hiding in my purse. Don't judge me. After all that running I deserved some fun!

WILD ADVENTURES

Finding adventure on the sand doesn't mean travelling to such an extreme and inhospitable desert. There are some exhilarating beach activities that will make you see the sand in a completely new way.

1 Beach CAMPFIRE

Not all beaches allow campfires, but if you have permission from the landowner, there's nothing better than chilling by a small fire next to the water. Ask an adult to help you build and light the fire. Never burn plastic. Ardwell Bay on the Galloway Peninsula in Scotland, and Nanjizal Beach at Land's End, are my favourite spots.

WARNING
Adult supervision required for adventures.

2 BEACH Running

Running on the sand is fantastic exercise so head to your nearest beach to try it. The uneven surface of the sand means you have to use the muscles in your feet and legs more, so you'll burn up lots of energy. Go barefoot for added adventure. I have feet as hard as trotters, so I'm normally the first person to kick off my shoes and wiggle my toes in the sand. Formby, Merseyside, has great dunes for adding some hill runs. Try making your own course and challenging your friends or family to a race.

3 Beach Galloping

There's nothing more epic than galloping on horseback down a deserted beach with the sea crashing beside you. Book a guide to show you the best route and to keep you safe. Holkham, Norfolk, and Lindisfarne, Northumberland, are both jaw-dropping.

KITE Landboarding

It is not for the faint-hearted, but kite landboarding is addictive. You stand on what is essentially a giant skateboard with thick wheels and use a kite to pull you across the sand. It works best on a flat and deserted beach because you will go far and fast. The trick is to keep your balance as you catch the wind and get enough power to propel yourself forwards. But too much power means you very quickly lose control and will go flying. North Norfolk is a great place to watch seriously skilled boarders do awesome tricks.

KITE LAND BOARDING
— Helen's Report —

I tried kite landboarding on a beach in Devon and it was the biggest adrenaline rush ever. I had no idea just how fast it was possible to go. With my feet firmly strapped to the board, I navigated the kite into the wind and began to move across the sand at speed. I had more than a few crashes and even ended up flying through the air at one point. Landboarding was without a doubt one of the best things I have ever attempted, even though sometimes I was going so fast I could hardly breathe. I was clinging to the kite for dear life, trying desperately to keep control of it. The feeling of excitement tingled down my back for hours afterwards. I loved it – and I also loved watching the professionals show off their mesmerizing skills.

WHERE to go WILD

Silecroft, England
With stunning scenery and quiet beaches this is the perfect place to go beach horse-riding.

Monte Kaolino, Germany
Try sand-skiing down different runs on this sand dune.

Huacachina, Peru
Sand dunes that stretch all the way to the shore of the Pacific Ocean make this an epic desert spot for sandboarding. It's top of my places-to-visit wish list.

5 Sandboarding

Sandboarding is very similar to snowboarding, but instead of riding down a snowy mountain, you weave down a sand dune. You can use a proper sandboard, a sledge or surfboard, and go down the dune standing, sitting or lying on the board. A helmet is essential. Unlike with snowboarding, there's no lift to take you to the top, so you'll get a good work-out scrambling back up the dunes to have another go. I wanted to try it in Swakopmund in Namibia, but my legs were too stiff after the race to get me to the top of the dune!

EXTREMELY WILD ADVENTURES

If you ever get a chance to visit one of the world's deserts, seize the opportunity to experience an otherworldly landscape.

1 SEE a DESERT SUNRISE

Camping overnight in a desert is an amazing experience: the big open skies and lack of light pollution makes star gazing sensational. Make sure you wake up at sunrise, or time your visit to be then. Watch as the sun breaks across the vast wilderness. Imagine how spectacular the Grand Canyon would look at first light.

2 VISIT a DESERT CITY

Although deserts might seem to be inhospitable, people have made their homes there for thousands of years. Visiting a desert city and walking around ruins that are thousands of years old is spellbinding.

3 GO on a CAMEL TREK

Camels are perhaps the best-known desert animal, with their cleverly adapted humps that allow them to go without food and water for long periods. For thousands of years, humans have used camels as a way to cross the desert. Dubai and Lanzarote are great places to meet camels. Trekking across the ridge of a sand dune with a guide is an amazing way to experience the desert up close.

SUNRISE DESERT YOGA ABU DHABI
– Helen's Report –

The Rub' al-Khali desert is the world's largest uninterrupted desert, covering parts of Saudi Arabia, Yemen, Oman and the United Arab Emirates. I was staying in Abu Dhabi in the United Arab Emirates and I visited Rub' al-Khali at sunrise to practise yoga. Yoga is an ancient form of exercise that helps build your core strength, flexibility and balance. I love it because it gives you a chance to stop, look, listen and breathe. Dawn in the desert was far colder than I had expected, but I was so grateful to experience the landscape in the early light and see the crazy colours of a desert sunrise. It was calm. Quiet. The way the light fell on the ripples in the sand and the shadows that the dunes cast was hypnotic. It was almost eerie how still it was. It was very humbling to be one small person in such a vast landscape.

WHERE to go WILD

Petra, Jordan
This ancient desert city, carved from pink sandstone, is over 2,000 years old.

Death Valley, USA
This desert valley holds the record for hottest air temperature, reaching 56.7°C in 1913. The 135-mile Badwater Ultra-Marathon goes through Death Valley. The ground is apparently hot enough to melt your trainers.

Outback, Australia
Discover epic rock formations with rock art dating from 20,000 years ago and desert that seems to stretch for ever.

WILD GIRL TOP TIP

If you're hot and you have access to ice, put an ice cube on your head under a hat so it slowly melts and drips down your neck. I've also been known to put ice cubes inside my underwear if I don't have my hands free to hold a cold compress. My armpits, groin, neck and head are the places I try to keep cool if I am worried about over-heating.

WILD GIRL Wall of Fame

These women have all achieved amazing feats of endurance across sweltering terrains.

Belinda KIRK

Belinda Kirk has searched for camels in China's Desert of Death and rock paintings in the mountains of Lesotho. She's also determined to help others bring more adventure into their lives. One of her most memorable adventures was leading a group of people with disabilities across Nicaragua. She is the founder of the Wild Night Out, an annual night of adventure in the UK.

Any woman who chooses to sky-dive to celebrate their 65th birthday deserves respect. Alpha Bennett started exercising in her 40s and by her 70s was competing in triathlons. She is a nationally ranked marathon runner in the USA.

ALPHA BENNETT

Cheryl Strayed

Aged 26, with no experience or training, Cheryl Strayed hiked by herself more than a thousand miles along the Pacific Crest Trail in the USA. She endured 40°C temperatures, record-breaking snowfall, rattlesnakes, bears and even losing a boot! The book about her adventure, *Wild*, was made into a film.

SARAH MARQUIS

Sarah Marquis walked alone from Siberia, in Russia, to Australia. In three years she crossed six countries, travelling through mountains, deserts and jungles.

JAX MARIASH

Nicknamed "Queen of the Desert", Jax Mariash is the first woman to complete the 4 Deserts Race Series Grand Slam Plus: four week-long endurance races across the Gobi Desert, the Sahara, the Atacama Crossing in Chile and the freezing deserts of Antarctica.

Robyn Davidson

Robyn Davidson solo trekked 1,700 miles across the remote deserts of west Australia, with a dog and four camels: Dookie, Bub, Zeleika and Goliath. *Tracks*, her book about the adventure, inspired a film.

INSERT PHOTO HERE

YOU!

WHERE WILL YOUR NEXT ADVENTURE TAKE YOU?

ADVENTURES

HELEN'S AMAZING AMAZON ADVENTURE

I grew up a short walk from the River Eden in Cumbria. I spent half my childhood on that river: paddling, swimming and building rafts. I never would have guessed that one day I would solo kayak over 2,000 miles of the Amazon, one of the greatest waterways in the world. I'd only been in a kayak a couple of times before taking on this charity challenge for television, so in truth, I didn't really know what to expect.

I had no idea the river would be over 10 miles wide in some parts. I underestimated the fact it crosses a whole continent. Maybe that's a good thing though. If I had known how big and dangerous the challenge was, would I have gone? People asked me if I was scared. I wasn't, but only because I didn't know what lay ahead.

Almost everyone told me I wouldn't make it and that the challenge was too hard, too dangerous and too ambitious. That only made me more determined to try. I didn't know if I would succeed. That's the thing about me though, and the thing I would say to you: if you don't think you can do it, try it anyway. The first time I got into a kayak in training, I fell out of the boat. However, I ended up with two kayaking World Records, not because I am skilled or hugely talented, but because I simply kept going. If you can find a way to block out what other people think and focus your energy on what you need to do, you might surprise yourself. I kayaked from dawn to dusk for forty-two days. Apart from a few hours here and there for filming, I just sat in that boat and paddled. And the people that doubted me at the start had turned into an army of supporters by the end.

If you are like me and prepared to take the plunge, there are so many different adventures you can have on the water. Just take a deep breath and dive in.

WILD WORLD

At over 4,000 miles in length, the Amazon is one of the world's greatest rivers. It winds its way through several South American countries, beginning in the Andes mountains in Peru, and eventually reaching the sea in Brazil.

Adventures on THE AMAZON

CHALLENGE: To solo kayak down the Amazon, starting in Peru and finishing where the river turns tidal in Brazil. I had under two months to paddle 2,000 miles, so I was going to be in the kayak from morning till night, whatever the weather.

SOUTH AMERICA

COLOMBIA

PERU

NAUTA
START

Leticia

Fonte Boa

Tefé

BRAZIL

MEANS OF TRANSPORT
Kayak

DISTANCE
2,010 miles
(the extra 10
miles took me
into Almeirim)

DAYS
42

MILES PER DAY
50 to 60 on average

TEMPERATURE
Highs of 31°C

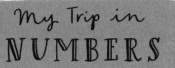

My Trip in
NUMBERS

1
million paddle strokes

2
injections for sickness

10
hours a day of paddling

6
days of paddling a week for 6 weeks

45
metres of medical tape used on
my hands to stop them blistering

2
Guinness World Records (both since broken)
for longest solo journey in a kayak and the
longest distance travelled in a kayak over
24 hours by a woman (75 miles)

N W E S

ALMEIRIM
FINISH

Oriximiná

Parintins

Santarém

MANAUS Itacoatiara

TRAINING and PREPARATION

When I signed up to solo kayak one of the world's biggest rivers, I hadn't been in a kayak since a school trip. This challenge was about more than physical ability though. It was going to be an experience that would test me in every possible way. People told me not to attempt the Amazon, but I was determined to give it everything. I trained as hard as I could in the four months leading up to the adventure.

The first time I got into a kayak in training, I went straight into the cold and murky river. I was lucky to have Mark Hoile as my coach, who was prepared to teach me the basics. When I started, I couldn't have told you the difference between a kayak and a canoe. I discovered that a kayak is a closed-top boat. The paddler is seated and uses a double-bladed paddle to move the boat through the water. In a canoe, the paddler kneels in the boat and uses a single-bladed paddle to propel the boat forwards. The team agreed that I should have the easiest and fastest boat possible. I was given a long, thin sea kayak, whom I named *Anne-Marie*.

Once I had a boat, I had to master the art of the stroke. Weirdly enough it's your stomach and legs that do most of the work when you are kayaking: your shoulders and arms transmit power, but the driving force comes from your legs. A good stroke relies on you twisting your torso and pushing through your legs and feet. I was surprised by how much my posture made a difference and I did weights in the gym to build my core strength.

I also needed to learn how to right a capsized kayak, a technique known as "rolling". You throw your head and torso underwater, then twist your body while you are upside down so you can snap back up into a sitting position. I confess I learned this important survival skill in a swimming pool. It seemed a much more appealing place to practise than a freezing lake in Cumbria in the middle of winter!

BEDROOM KAYAK PRACTICE

When I wasn't training on the water or paddling machine, I practised my paddling technique sitting on my bed at home.

1 Sit on your bed, with your legs stretched out in front of you. Grab your paddle (you can also use a broom or mop).

3 Pull the blade of the paddle alongside the "kayak" (the edge of the bed) towards your hip.

2 Put one end of your paddle into the "water" (the space off the bed) by your toes. Keep your front arm almost straight. Your wrist will be level with your eyes. Ideally you want your knees to bend slightly upwards and outwards and your heels should be angled towards the centre of the kayak.

4 Lift the blade out of the water and immediately repeat the same action on the other side.

TRAINING TIMELINE

I didn't dare take any time off from training in the four months leading up to the adventure. When I couldn't get out on the water, I trained on a paddling machine called an Ergometer. I spent hour after hour paddling on the Ergo in my living room and I even took it with me when I was travelling around the country, so I could paddle wherever I was. Sometimes Mark would boil two kettles to make the room steamy, and give me a taste of what it would be like to paddle through the intense heat.

KIT LIST

The kayak was my most important piece of kit. I also needed to be sure I was prepared for the hot and wet Amazon climate. As I had a support boat sailing beside me, I only had to take on board what I needed for that day of paddling. These were my essentials.

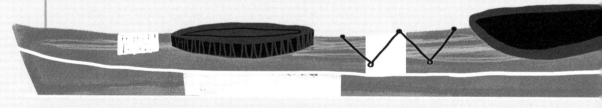

PADDLE

KAYAK

I loved my sea kayak. We took a spare boat just in case, but I never enjoyed being in anything other than the *Anne-Marie*. I named the boat after my friend Anne-Marie, who planned the whole trip and deserved the credit.

GLOVES

The paddle rubbed the sensitive bits of my hands. As my skin was constantly wet it would blister if not protected.

SUNGLASSES

It was sunny and there was glare off the water. I had wrap-around glasses that didn't let any light in at the sides, top or bottom.

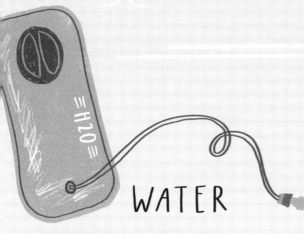

WATER

Because I was sweating so much, I needed to keep drinking water. I had a water pouch with a hose that I clipped on to my top so that I could drink without having to stop paddling.

FOOD

I needed the calories for energy, but sickness stopped me wanting to eat. I ate a lot of rice and bananas. At night there was freshly caught fish, mainly from fishermen whom I paddled past.

ANNE-MARIE

SUNCREAM

sun cream

I was practically bathing in factor 50 suncream. I was worried that if I wasn't careful, sunburn could end my challenge.

WIDE-BRIMMED HAT

Paddling all day in the heat was dangerous so a hat to protect my head was essential.

Sure, I saw toucans and sloths every day, but I also weed and threw up on myself countless times. There were good times and bad times, which I guess is the best way to describe almost two months kayaking down one of the world's biggest and most dangerous rivers. I never knew what each day would bring – and that made it exciting.

ARRIVING AT THE AMAZON

I was setting off from Nauta in Peru, the point at which two rivers meet to form the Amazon. Getting to the nearest town involved two flights, the latter full of explorers laden down with heavy backpacks. I saw the Amazon from the sky, the brown river snaking its way through dense rainforest, and for the first time the enormity of what I was trying to achieve sank in.

The first challenge was getting the kayak from the airport to the river. In the end we had to load it onto a tuk tuk and send it down a busy road. Then it took a while to locate the crew's support boat. Logistics are the key to having a successful trip, and I will be for ever grateful to my teammates whose careful planning made my adventure possible.

THE BUILD UP

I had never felt so anxious before an adventure. It wasn't so much anxiety about what I had to do, but about all the things that needed to fall into place for the challenge to be a success. The weather had to be good. I couldn't get ill with yellow fever or malaria. The anacondas had to stay away from my boat. All the risks I was being constantly reminded of ate into my excitement. I was mentally exhausted before I had even started paddling, which was not a great way to begin.

PADDLING PLAN

All I actually had to do was paddle. One stroke after another, again and again. We divided the distance by the number of days and worked out I needed to do about 60 miles a day. That was further than I had paddled in training and the maths didn't allow for things to go wrong. The crew believed in me and I didn't want to let them down.

It was 3.30 a.m. and pitch black when I first encountered the Amazon. I got into my kayak, feeling incredibly small on the vast expanse of water. As it got light, I realized that the river was so wide that often I couldn't see the bank on the other side. And I wasn't prepared for the boats passing me on the river. Thunderous ferries and giant tankers created waves that soaked me and made my little boat bounce around.

HIGHS and LOWS

I cried almost every day I was on the river. Sometimes it was from laughter, other times it was because I felt completely overwhelmed. The conditions constantly changed, so it was hard to even plan a route. The water was so brown, that most of the time I couldn't see the paddle once it broke the surface. Sometimes the flow of the river was slow like melted chocolate, but after a storm it became more like a conveyor belt of water lilies, huge logs and even the odd flip-flop.

Most days I was on the water for 10 hours at a time. I would wake in the dark and eat as much breakfast as I could. Then I would get in the kayak and start paddling. A lot of the time, all I had to look at was the vast sky. For the first few hours my arms and shoulders were stiff as I warmed up, and then the pain in my bum and legs would take over. My lips were constantly sunburned. Occasionally I would pause to eat a bowl of rice or to rest when the heat got too intense. I would stop paddling when it was dark, then eat and sleep on the support boat. I went six days at a time without putting my feet on dry land.

LIFE ON THE RIVER

I couldn't just let the current carry me. I had to be ready to paddle into the fastest bits and avoid the slow bits or streams that might send me back in a circle. I had to stay out of the way of boats, logs and anything that would damage me or my boat. My iPod broke on the second day, so I played games with myself, going through the alphabet to keep my mind occupied.

I knew I wouldn't want to be getting in and out of the boat when I needed to wee or poo, as I would lose valuable time. I did the odd wee in the boat and just washed it out. There was so much river water swilling around it didn't really matter! For poos, I would hang out of the back of the boat. It took strength to hang on and balance but I managed.

The blisters on my hands and bum became a daily reminder that I wasn't used to the conditions. I missed warm showers. I missed my family. Each day I would colour in the section of river I had completed on the map. It seemed so small and insignificant that in the end my friends, Eric, Gav, Stu, Lucy and Ben, folded the map in half, so I couldn't see how far I had to go. I could only see what I had done.

THE CONDITIONS

I learned to take the challenge day by day. I told myself that after a low comes a high. Whatever was making me cry might make me laugh in an hour and usually it did. What kept me going were the words of encouragement I got from my family, friends and the public who really got behind the challenge. The best part was not knowing what each day would bring. What could be more exciting than being on a river full of deadly fish and dangerous pirates?

SURF THE AMAZON

Imagine surfing for miles up the world's largest river. That's what surfers from all over the world are doing thanks to a rare but natural phenomenon called a tidal bore. The bore, known in Brazil as Pororoca, happens when the incoming ocean tide creates an influx of water into the river, and forms a big wave that can be surfed for miles.

DANGER ZONE!

Even though all I had to do was sit in the kayak and paddle, there was still plenty that could – and did – go wrong.

BLISTERS

I admit that it was stupid to only bring one pair of kayaking gloves on a six-week kayaking trip. The thumbs of my gloves quickly became threadbare and blisters began to bubble under the skin of my hands. To stop the blisters getting worse, the team doctor had to tape up each of my fingers every morning. Sitting in wet clothes on the hard kayak seat for so many hours also meant I got sores on my hips and bum.

HEAT EXHAUSTION

At the beginning of the trip, I wasn't drinking enough water to replace the water I was losing as sweat. I knew I was suffering from heat exhaustion when I started feeling sick towards the end of a long day in the first week. I couldn't stop retching and my head was throbbing. I needed anti-sickness injections in my bum. I learned an important lesson: I had to drink before I got thirsty and take breaks in the shade when it got too hot.

RIVER SICKNESS

My kayak was tiny compared to some of the enormous boats on the river: some were big enough to carry massive lorries. These big boats would churn up the water behind them. A lot of the time, I would be paddling through choppy water and it was almost impossible not to get splashes of water in my mouth. The water was dirty, full of all kinds of bacteria, and this combined with the bumpy motion made me pretty sick at times. Yet because of my mileage target, I couldn't stop to rest. I learned the hard way that if I tried to throw up over the side, I would unbalance the kayak and capsize into my own sick. I had little choice but to aim forwards. A few times I literally threw up all over myself. Afterwards I would wash the sick off with river water and just keep paddling.

STORMS

My progress depended on the weather. Most of the time it was hot and sticky, and often it was so windy I struggled to sit upright in the kayak. Occasionally there would be storms so savage I thought the world would end. I would watch the storm roll down the river towards me. The first giveaway would be the smell. Then it would go eerily quiet until thick cloud crept up the river accompanied by a thunderous roar. Within minutes, raindrops would be falling, as big as pebbles and as painful as tennis balls. The wind would practically push me backwards, making it impossible to paddle. On those days I had to admit defeat and retreat to the support boat. Even then I loved the storms. The fresh rain was heavenly after days of sticky heat. To be at the mercy of the weather was very humbling and a reminder that humans have far less power than we think we do.

POLICE AND PIRATES

On the border between Peru and Colombia, in an unexpected and dramatic twist, armed policemen stormed our boat as they weren't happy with our travel documents. We had to leave the river to go to the local police station and wait for it to be sorted out. In Brazil, we had the threat of pirates, known as "water rats", to worry about. These gangs of armed men rob boats and have been known to murder people in their raids. For safety on some nights, we didn't sleep on the support boat but moored up and stayed with families who lived on the riverbank.

The AMAZON

For six weeks my view was water, sky and rainforest. The Amazon Basin is an unbelievable place, teeming with so many different kinds of animals and plants. There was the scorpion and tarantula that both made it inside my boat, the dolphins that swam beside my kayak and the monkeys that howled in the rainforest trees. I fell in love with the Amazon and was lucky to get to experience it in such a unique way.

Usually I slept on the support boat with the team, but I wanted to experience the rainforest. We hung hammocks between the trees and camped out one night. It was one of the most memorable experiences of my life. Walking into the forest was intense. The trees were taller than anything I had ever seen before. They

seemed to go on for miles, stretching into the sky in a dense canopy of leaves and foliage. The sun was so strong that it broke through the thick canopy, sending bright beams of light down to the dark jungle floor, like a torch breaking through a dark night. The air was warm and moist and it felt as though a heavy energy-sapping duvet was wrapped around me. There was no breeze, just hot, humid air.

The AMAZING AMAZON

🌺 The Amazon Basin is the area of land drained by the Amazon River and the smaller rivers that feed it. Most of the basin is covered by the Amazon rainforest.

🌺 The Amazon rainforest crosses nine South American countries — Brazil, Bolivia, Peru, Colombia, Ecuador, Venezuela, Guyana, Suriname and French Guiana.

🌺 The Amazon is the world's largest tropical rainforest, covering over 2.6 million square miles. If it were a country, it would be the ninth largest country in the world.

🌺 Several million species of animals, insects, birds and plants are found in the Amazon Basin. The area is home to more than 10% of all plant and animal species known on Earth.

What you see can't top what you hear. The noises in the Amazon rainforest are incredible: constant, unidentifiable, changing and intriguing. It is impossible to say what you're listening to, as there's a mix of creaks, clicks, groans and howls. Some are spooky, some are funny. Some of the monkey cackles and wails were so loud, I would have sworn the animals were metres from my head. We were assured by our guide that they were miles away.

Hammocks are brilliant because they keep you off the ground and away from anything that might nibble on you, but they are so hard to get into. I must have landed on the floor in a pile three times before I actually managed to balance in one. Even then it was hard to sleep because there was so much going on. The creaks and clicks were constant, and as my eyes got used to the dark, I was mesmerized by the moving shadows of the leaves. It's funny how your mind plays tricks on you when you're tired and hungry.

ANIMAL ALERT

Everyone kept saying: "Aren't you scared of the spiders, the snakes or the flesh-eating fish?" In truth, I wasn't. Some of the world's most rare and intriguing animals live in the Amazon and I was excited to be getting up close and personal with some incredible species.

MOSQUITO

It seems odd in an environment full of big and fearsome predators that small insects can actually pose the most danger. Mosquitos thrive in hot and humid tropical environments, and carry diseases including yellow fever and malaria. They feasted on me in the kayak, where they were protected from the wind. I couldn't fight them off, given my hands were full with the paddle. My feet were covered in red and itchy bites, and they had sucked my blood, but luckily I didn't get ill.

PINK RIVER DOLPHIN (or Amazon River Dolphin)

The pink river dolphin is one of three species of dolphin that only live in fresh water. These distinctive animals are an unusual pink colour, with long snouts and big round heads. On Valentine's Day, I found myself in the middle of about six pairs of river dolphins. They were jumping over each other and bobbing their noses out of the water inches from my kayak to say hello. It was without a doubt one of the most unbelievable things I have ever seen.

BLACK CAIMAN

This alligator-like creature has jaws capable of breaking a human's arm in a single snap. Other smaller caiman species sometimes swam alongside my kayak.

SLOTH

Sloths are so slow they will live in the same tree for years. Algae grow on their coats which gives them extra camouflage, making their greyish hair appear slightly green.

HYACINTH MACAW

The bright blue parrots were one of the most beautiful birds I saw in the rainforest.

HOWLER MONKEY

The cry of the howler monkey carries for miles. I loved listening out for them.

GREEN ANACONDA

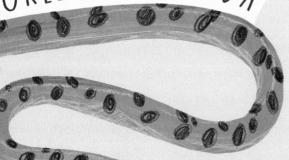

Green anacondas are one of the most revered species of the Amazon and the largest snakes in the world. They live in the Amazon's swamps and slow-moving streams, where they remain submerged in the water, waiting to strike. They catch their prey within their lethal coils, then swallow it whole.

JAGUAR

I obviously wouldn't have wanted to be nose-to-nose with a jaguar, but I would have loved to have caught a glimpse of one of these glorious rainforest-dwelling cats. They are the third largest big cat species after the tiger and the lion, and kill their prey using suffocation and a powerful bite.

PIRANHA

Piranhas are infamous for their powerful jaws and razor-sharp teeth. Their bite can easily tear through flesh.

Adventure REPORT

Staring at the Amazon sky for six weeks really was the best of times and the worst of times. It was a once in a lifetime adventure, and I was silly because at times I let the pressure get on top of me. I was so worried about the mileage, I didn't always take in the experience. My friend, Eric, told me not to wish it away. He was right. As I paddled that final mile, I realized the amazing days had hugely outnumbered the hard days.

The thing I didn't fully appreciate before that trip was how important family is. I don't mean your parents or your siblings, as fabulous as they are (and mine are off-the-scale fabulous). I mean the family you create around you, wherever you are. Yes I was in that kayak by myself, but on that river I was part of a much bigger team. A team that motivated me, helped me eat, taped up my fingers, covered me in suncream and wiped sick from my face. I wanted to smash the mileage target because I didn't want them to be disappointed.

Never underestimate the value of surrounding yourself with good people. People who will tell you that anything is possible, but will also keep your feet on the ground. People who support you but tell you when you are acting like an idiot. People who can make you laugh, even when you're on a river in the middle of nowhere, surrounded by caimans, with only rice to eat and so exhausted you can hardly move. And, wow, did those guys make me laugh. Without that laughter I couldn't and wouldn't have done it.

BEST BITS

1 The sunsets and sunrises. I didn't think I could spend so long looking at the same view. I spent hours and weeks looking at the horizon and it was a privilege to see the sun rise and fall so many times in such an epic part of the world.

WORST BITS

1 Dunking my iPod in the river. I learned the lyrics of every song on JLS's first album. It was the only thing my iPod would play after it got wet.

2 Being away from everyone and everything. So many times I thought: "I wish my parents could see this." It's great seeing amazing things but seeing them with people you love is even better.

3 The blisters. My hands were a mess and never really got better because they were constantly wet and rubbing.

4 The chocolate. We picked up treats at stalls in villages we saw every week and the chocolate we found was never as tasty as I wanted it to be.

2 The wildlife. The kayak brought me close to so many unbelievable things. Having river dolphins and even caimans swim beside me was awesome.

3 The fishermen who would approach us on speed boats and try to sell us fish or buy coffee or sugar from us. It beats going to the supermarket.

4 The family who paddled out to meet me. A Peruvian family had seen me on television, trying to explain in broken Portuguese what I was doing, and they were so amused they came out to see if I was real!

LAND LEGS

On the few occasions we stopped and went into a village or town to film or for supplies, I remember putting on flip-flops and walking on solid, dry ground. I couldn't believe how weird it felt at first. I was so used to walking on a boat that was constantly moving, or sitting in my kayak, that to be standing fully upright on solid ground was nothing short of odd.

RAINFOREST HOMESTAY

I loved the night we stayed with a family on the edge of the rainforest in a huge house on stilts. I say house, but it was more like a maze of rooms and platforms with connecting walkways between them made from planks.

WILD ADVENTURES

The Amazon is a remote and extreme place and you don't need to go that far to experience the adrenaline rush of the water. There are adventures to be had in rivers, lakes or the sea. There's no excuse not to get your toes wet.

1 BUILD a RAFT and FLOAT down a RIVER

All you need is a wooden pallet, two empty plastic drums, lots of rope and a patient parent or adult to supervise. When my brother and I were young we used to build a raft and take it on our grandad's pick-up truck down to the river. We would float, capsize and swim downstream until our parents could fish us out. Wear a buoyancy aid and old trainers, so you don't stub your toes on stones.

2 GHYLL Scrambling

Ghyll scrambling is when you travel up or down a mountain stream. Book a guide so you can explore ancient gorges, abseil down waterfalls, jump into deep plunge pools and scramble up waterfalls. You'll need sensible shoes, a wetsuit, helmet and buoyancy aid.

3 DRAGON BOAT RACING

Dragon boat racing originated in ancient China and is becoming a popular team sport on rivers everywhere. A crew is normally twenty-two people strong and the paddlers sit in ten rows. The steerer controls the boat and the drummer sets the pace. You need to be in sync with your partner and the rest of the team. The pace is generally set by the pair at the front of the boat, and the aim is that everyone's paddles enter and exit the water at the same time. I used to paddle with an all girls' team on the Thames in London and I learned that you need good rhythm and strong arms.

4 SURFING

Learn to catch waves on a surfboard. It takes strength, balance and practice to be able to stand up and stay upright, but it is totally worth it for how cool you will feel.

5 STAND-UP PADDLE BOARDING

Stand-up paddle boarding (SUP) is a bit like surfing, but the board is much bigger and you stand up on it, using a paddle to propel the board through the water. You can do it on flat, calm water (my favourite) or surf waves in the sea. There are hundreds of places across the world where you can hire a board.

6 KITE-Surfing

Kite-surfing is similar to kite-skiing: you use the power of a kite to pull you through the waves. I learned in Devon, where I face-planted a lot but I loved it, despite the bruises. The kites are strong enough to whip you out of the water and send you through the air on your board, but the feeling is as close to flying as you are likely to get.

WHERE to go WILD

Cornwall, England
The crashing waves of the Atlantic mean you can kayak and surf to your heart's content.

Exmouth, England
Where to start: there's paddle boarding, windsurfing, kite-surfing and an army of qualified instructors.

Collioure, France
My favourite place for stand-up paddle boarding.

Nabq Bay, Egypt
There's brilliant kite-surfing and snorkelling on this beach.

WARNING
Adult supervision required for adventures.

EXTREMELY WILD ADVENTURES

Take the plunge with these extremely wild adventures.

1 WILD SWIMMING

Wild swimming is outdoor swimming in lakes, rivers and the sea – any body of natural water that takes your fancy. It's hard to say what's so good about it, and in my experience you either like it or you don't. I LOVE it. It makes me feel amazing afterwards: like there's a shot of energy running through me. If you try wild swimming, remember it can be dangerous so you need an adult with you. Give your body time to get used to the cold and be aware of deep water and currents.

LAKE ULLSWATER in the LAKE DISTRICT
– Helen's Report –

Lake Ullswater in the Lake District is cold. So cold it never fails to make me gasp, but that's what makes swimming in it so invigorating and so fun. I have an inflatable kayak which I paddle out to the middle of Ullswater, then I jump off for a swim. Once I've got over the initial shock of the water, it is the best way to see the surrounding fells.

2 KAYAK or CANOE ADVENTURE

You can have an incredible adventure in a canoe or a kayak. Go with a guide who can show you secret spots or amazing wildlife on rivers, lakes or the sea – I saw whales in Canada. Make sure you have a buoyancy aid, a paddle, a bailer in case you take on water and sensible shoes.

3 ROCK JUMPING

Adrenaline junkies will be well aware of the phenomenon that is cliff jumping. Some people call it tombstoning. Cliff jumping is simple: you don't need equipment or special clothing. That doesn't mean it isn't very dangerous and you must do it with an adult's permission and with their supervision at all times. After all, you are jumping from a rock into the water. It is terrifying and exciting in equal measure. You must always check the water is deep enough before jumping in and be careful of any submerged rocks and strong currents. Start small to begin with and never jump before you are ready. Make your body as streamlined as possible as you jump. Do not be fooled into thinking water offers a soft landing. I have learned the hard way, if you enter the water badly, it hurts. Take your time and never do anything you aren't comfortable with. Know your limits and don't be distracted by others.

WARNING
Adult supervision required for adventures.

4 COASTEERING

Coasteering involves scrambling around the rocky coastline and jumping off cliffs into the sea. (Not every coasteering trip involves cliff jumping – there are plenty of routes that don't require a head for heights.) I recommend joining a group or an organized tour. You'll get given the necessary helmet, buoyancy aid and wetsuit and you'll have the benefit of local knowledge of the best routes and wildlife-watching spots.

WHERE to go WILD

Lee Valley White Water Centre, England
A great place to hone your canoe and kayak skills.

Lake District, England
From white-water rivers to calm lakes for wild swimming, there is something for everyone.

Pembrokeshire, Wales
A beautiful coasteering spot.

Cala en Brut, Menorca
There are lots of rocky platforms, perfect for jumping into the sea.

WILD GIRL TOP TIP

One-piece swimming costumes are a much better option than bikinis, which can fly off in the water. If you are climbing over rocks or on a pebble beach, old trainers or wetsuit boots will protect your feet.

WILD GIRL Wall of Fame

Get on board with these women's wild adventures on the water.

TEAM ANTIGUA
Island Girls

Team Antigua Island Girls are the first black rowing team to cross any ocean. As part of the Talisker Whisky Atlantic Challenge, they rowed 3,000 miles across the Atlantic.

Lizzie Carr is the first person to paddle board the entire length of Britain's waterways. Her 400-mile journey took 22 days and inspired her to start the #PlasticPatrol campaign. Lizzie is the first person to paddle board the entire length of the Hudson River in New York.

LIZZIE CARR

Sylvia Earle

Oceanographer and explorer Dr Sylvia Earle became the first woman to walk untethered on the ocean floor, 381 metres below the surface in 1979. Her World-Record breaking walk, off the coast of Oahu, Hawaii, lasted over 2 hours!

SARAH OUTEN

In her London2London adventure, Sarah Outen looped the planet using a rowing boat, bike and kayak. It took her over 4 years to cover 25,000 miles and twice she had to be rescued from hurricanes.

AUGUST 2007

THE SISTERHOOD

The 18-strong Sisterhood became the fastest and first all-female crew to Dragon Boat across the English Channel, completing the crossing in just 3 hours 42 minutes.

Hilary Lister was the first quadriplegic woman to sail solo around Britain. She was paralysed from the neck down so controlled her yacht by blowing into three different straws. One of her highlights was seeing whales breach in the ocean beside her.

HILARY
Lister

INSERT
PHOTO
HERE

YOU!

WHERE WILL YOUR NEXT
ADVENTURE TAKE YOU?

ADVENTURES

I grew up in the countryside, far away from any cities. On one side of our house were the fells of the Lake District. On the other side, where my bedroom was, there were the Pennines. If I'm honest, at times I found it lonely. It's only as I've got a bit older, I've realized just how important wide open spaces are to me. I never feel as free as I do when I'm up a mountain, where you can dance, run, walk or skip. You can be whoever you want to be.

You can have so many different adventures in the mountains, walking, running or climbing. You can wriggle through gaps in them. Fly over them. Cycle down them. Adventures can last hours, days or weeks. Mountains change colour as the seasons unfold. They are dangerous and exciting and have to be treated with respect at all times.

Being Cumbrian, my heart will always belong to the Lake District fells. Adventurers love to challenge themselves by climbing high and difficult mountains. For me it has never been about seeing how high I could climb. Mountains are about fun and freedom, and appreciating the landscape. I climbed Ben Nevis, the highest mountain in the UK, with a huge group of girlfriends. Some of the girls had run back-to-back marathons. Others had never done any hill-walking before. Although it was tough at times, I loved every moment of it and it was incredible to have done it as part of a team.

Few people grow up surrounded by mountains, and there are so many other ways you can experience the buzz of walking or climbing. However you explore the wilderness, you'll soon discover how exciting the middle of nowhere can be.

WILD WORLD

Ben Nevis, in the northwest of the Scottish Highlands, is the highest mountain in Great Britain at 1,345 metres high. Once an active volcano, it is now a favourite destination for walkers and climbers, as there are so many different routes to the summit.

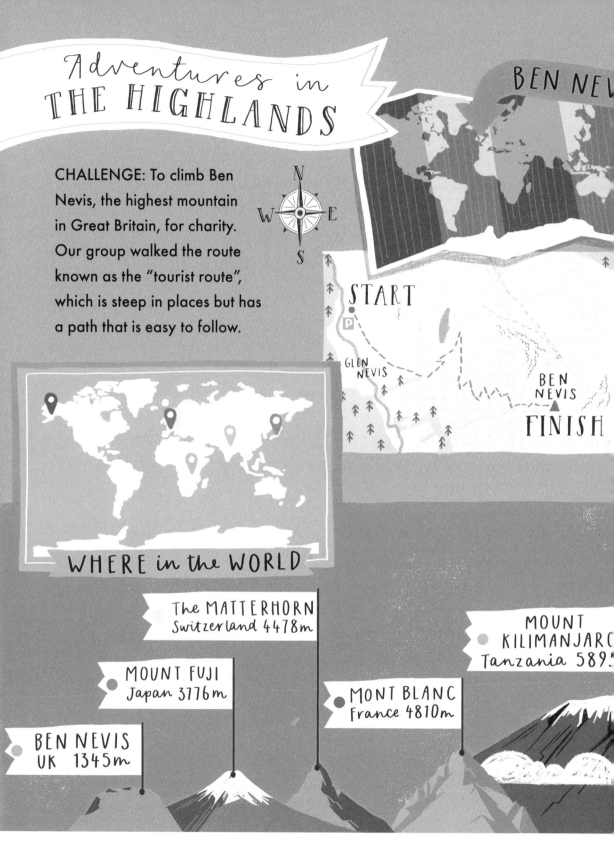

Adventures in THE HIGHLANDS

CHALLENGE: To climb Ben Nevis, the highest mountain in Great Britain, for charity. Our group walked the route known as the "tourist route", which is steep in places but has a path that is easy to follow.

BEN NEV

START

GLEN NEVIS

BEN NEVIS
FINISH

WHERE in the WORLD

The MATTERHORN
Switzerland 4478m

MOUNT KILIMANJARO
Tanzania 5895

MOUNT FUJI
Japan 3776m

MONT BLANC
France 4810m

BEN NEVIS
UK 1345m

HOW DOES BEN NEVIS COMPARE TO OTHER MOUNTAINS?

MEANS OF TRANSPORT
Foot

HEIGHT
1,345 metres

DISTANCE
10.5 miles

TIME
Around 3.5 to 5 hours
to get to the summit

TEMPERATURE
-1°C to -9°C at summit

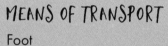

EVEREST
Nepal 8848m

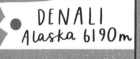

DENALI
Alaska 6190m

TRAINING and PREPARATION

I find a big walking challenge one of the nicest adventures to train for, because the preparation is so simple: you just walk everywhere! You don't need to go to the gym, you just walk with anyone, anywhere, pretty much in any weather.

I trained for Ben Nevis with early morning walks along the canal tow path near my house. I couldn't tell you how many miles I walked or how long it took me. I just based my training on a route I wanted to do that day. When I run, I listen to music, because I need the motivation, but when I'm walking I prefer to listen to my surroundings and let my mind wander.

One thing I will say is never underestimate the need to wear in your hiking boots before a big walk. New boots, or boots you haven't worn for a while, can give you blisters and end your challenge. For Ben Nevis, I wore my hiking boots every day in the weeks running up to our climb. Rather than walking the dog in trainers, I wore my boots, so I could set off for certain knowing the boots would not rub.

If you're going up a mountain, it's important to take food, water, wet-weather clothing and safety gear. It's also a good idea to get used to your rucksack, as you don't want the straps to rub and give you sore shoulders. As the climb got closer, on my morning walks I packed my rucksack with all the

MOUNTAIN ESSENTIALS

There is so much technology available you might think there is no need to learn to use a compass and a map. After all, we have phones and GPS devices that do pretty much the same job. However, a compass and a map are reliable: they won't run out of battery and they are unlikely to break. They may even save your life.

1 MAP

If you get lost or the weather changes, you need to be able to navigate your way to safety. Make sure you pick the right kind of map for the area. It should show roads, places of interest, waterways, wooded areas and landscape features, including all important contour lines which show how steep a hill or valley is.

2 COMPASS

Being able to use a compass is another essential navigation skill. A compass uses the Earth's magnetic field to find north, so you can find your way through cloud and fog.

3 WEATHER

The weather changes quickly on a mountain and the higher you climb, the colder it gets. Check the forecast before you begin (there are lots of different apps). Even more essential is that you have kit for all weathers, even if the sun is shining when you set off.

kit and water I was planning on carrying, so I could get used to the weight.

I think the hardest thing about training for a climb like Ben Nevis is getting your head in good shape. Although walking is something we do every day, it isn't always easy. Parts might be physically challenging or you might be at the back of the group. That's when you need to stay positive, which can be hard to do in a tough situation. Practise seeing the good in a situation. Practise laughing when you really want to cry. Repeat the phrase: "After a bad time there is always a good time." After all, one mile might be tough, but the next might be a piece of cake.

CHOOSING THE RIGHT ROUTE

People are killed on Ben Nevis every year, usually after getting caught in bad weather or from climbing accidents. As we were a big group and all had different levels of experience, we decided to follow the route known as the tourist route. Some people will tell you that this route is too busy (at least 125,000 people summit Ben Nevis every year) or that it doesn't show the mountain at its best. It's true that there are other incredibly challenging routes that will take you to the summit. However, if you don't have much mountaineering experience and you want to do it on foot and without a guide, the tourist route is easy to follow and makes the climb achievable. That doesn't mean you can forget any of your mountain essentials though.

KIT LIST

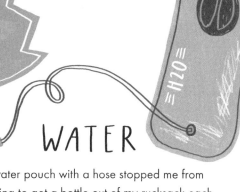

I only took a small rucksack with me when I climbed Ben Nevis, so it was important that I packed sensibly and made sure I had kit suitable for all weathers.

WATER

A water pouch with a hose stopped me from having to get a bottle out of my rucksack each time I wanted a drink. If it's hot and I'm likely to sweat, I also take a sachet of rehydration salts, so I don't get dehydrated.

HIKING BOOTS

Hiking boots are essential as they are sturdier and have more grip than trainers. They also give all-important ankle support, which is vital when climbing over uneven surfaces or coming downhill.

BLISTER PLASTERS

If I feel a burning or rubbing sensation anywhere on my foot or ankle, I've learned to put a blister plaster on. Prevention is better than cure.

HAT & GLOVES

Always protect the extremities.

PHONE

Never rely on a phone, as it might break or have no signal, but if taking one, make sure it is fully charged.

WATERPROOF JACKET & TROUSERS

It is essential to be prepared for wet weather. Getting wet means getting cold and the situation can quickly turn dangerous.

SUNCREAM

Even if it's not sunny, the face and any exposed parts of the body will get battered by the elements. All-weather suncream will stop wind-burn.

SNACKS

I took a mix of sweet and savoury, as I didn't know what I would fancy.

FLEECE

I always have a spare warm layer with me. It will be colder at the mountain top than at the bottom.

WHISTLE

To attract attention in an emergency.

RUCKSACK

An ideal day pack is about 35 litres. I spent time adjusting the straps so it was comfortable on my back and I tried not to make it unnecessarily heavy.

SMALL FIRST-AID KIT

Take the essentials.

MAP & COMPASS

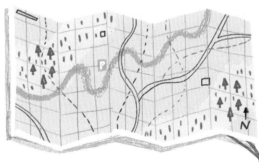

I always study the route before setting off. Getting a sense of any landmarks is a good motivator and gives me a sense of how far I have to go.

HEAD TORCH

A way to light the route if something goes wrong.

my HIGHLANDS DIARY

I climbed Ben Nevis one gorgeous day in July. Of all the challenges and adventures I have been lucky enough to be part of, this was different because I was in such a big group. I wasn't on my own and didn't have to motivate myself. I could enjoy being with my girlfriends and soaking up the amazing team spirit.

We started the ascent at about 8.30 a.m. at the Ben Nevis Visitor Centre. It was my birthday, so I was doubly excited about the day. The path was packed with walkers making the most of the good weather. Some people were head-to-toe in technical walking gear. Others were in normal clothes. Some had walking poles, some had dogs. There was someone from every walk of life on that path and the atmosphere was brilliant.

At first, the track was framed by trees, so we didn't really know what we were in for – in a good way. Then the path opened up and got steeper. A walk up a mountain is often toughest at the start. In a lot of cases, you go from walking on flat ground to climbing a very steep incline in a matter of metres. When the path became a series of rocky steps, I had to lift my knee high and use my arms to keep up the momentum. It was tiring work.

One of the girls in our group, Vicki, had never done any walking before and was finding the experience overwhelming. I reminded her it wasn't going to get easier until we were on our way down, but all she had to do was keep putting one foot in front of the other. She was finding it hard, but she didn't stop. She didn't make any excuses and she didn't quit. She was my hero for that.

GROUP GOALS

If you are in a group, you are part of a team. You might be one of the fastest or you might be one of the slowest. Either way it is very important that the team supports and encourages each other. It is terrible for team morale – and potentially dangerous – if the fast people charge off, leaving the slower members by themselves. Always stick together and look after each other. If you are towards the back of the group, remember that it is not a race. The most important thing is not to give up when the going gets tough.

DANGER ZONE!
SCREE

Scree is the broken fragments of rock that often form on slopes of a mountain. It can be dangerous because it is so slippery and if you misjudge your footing the ground can slide out from underneath you. Take it slowly and carefully, particularly if you are coming downhill.

We were so lucky with the weather that day. I have friends who have set off to climb Ben Nevis and have had to turn around because of bad weather. The danger for us was dehydration and sunburn, not something you often can say about Scotland. It is also important to eat before you get hungry so you keep your energy levels up. Dried fruit, nuts and cereal bars are all good. A lot of people recommend gels but be careful, as the sugar can be bad for your teeth. (That said, you can't beat a Tangfastic or ten when you're having an energy dip.)

Eventually the path levelled out. Before long we had reached a plateau that holds Loch Meall an t-Suidhe, known as the halfway lochan. It's not really halfway, but it's a good place to stop for a snack and enjoy the views. After the loch, the path climbs once more, and the terrain becomes rougher. There was a lot of scree on the final part of the ascent and I had to watch my footing.

It was a great feeling to reach the summit plateau. I'll never forget Vicki's face when she realized we could finally stop climbing. At the top the temperature was below freezing, even though it was July. We didn't hang around for long before beginning our descent.

After the sunshine on the way up it was baffling seeing a light dusting of snow lying across the summit plateau. We immediately had to put on our warm layers. Crossing the plateau to the summit marker, we passed many cairns. There are the remains of an observatory and a mountain rescue post too. The sweeping views

DANGER ZONE!
CLIFFS

The cliffs on the north side of Ben Nevis are among the highest in the UK. They have some of the best scrambles and rock climbs at all levels of difficulty. In winter, they are one of the principal locations in the UK for ice climbing. The path runs very close to the edge of the cliffs: take care if visibility is poor and do not approach the cliffs if there is snow on the top. There could be overhanging ledges which will collapse if you step on them.

CAIRNS

A cairn is a man-made pile of stones used to mark paths and help walkers navigate when the visibility is poor or the path is covered in snow. The cairns on the top of Ben Nevis are important as they guide walkers well away from the edges of the cliffs. If you see a cairn on a mountain, it is important to respect it. Don't use it as a place to bury rubbish or add stones to it.

across the Highlands were stunning, but for me the real drama was peering down the massive cliffs on the north side of the mountain. I loved watching the rock climbers working their way up the face. They make something so hard look so easy.

Climbing down Ben Nevis is easier going, but not pain free. It might be easier on your lungs but it's not easier on your knees, which take most of the impact. Take it slow and walk in single file. If you hurtle down as a big group, you could easily crash into people on the ascent. You also want to avoid twisting an ankle by stumbling over scree or rocks, especially when you are coming off the top.

On the way down, I loved noticing things I had missed because I was puffing and panting on the way up. Reaching the Visitor Centre at the bottom was bliss. There is no way to explain the satisfaction of turning back and looking up at a monumental mountain you have just conquered. You'll just have to try it!

Adventure REPORT

Not all adventures need to leave you feeling broken or battling the elements. I loved that climb up Ben Nevis because it was challenging enough to feel like we had achieved something but I never worried we would fail. I was really proud we got to the top and buzzing from the atmosphere.

An experience in a big group like this really shows that a challenge is relative: for some people running a mile is massive. For others, a marathon is a huge achievement. No challenge is more impressive than another, not in my eyes. To me, anyone who tackles something that is daunting, who goes beyond what they think they are capable of, is a winner. The most important thing is to get out of your comfort zone and have a go.

BEST BITS

1 To be able to climb Ben Nevis on such a beautiful sunny day with clear views was a privilege.

WORST BITS

1 Keeping my balance on the slippery scree. It's a scary feeling when you think you might fall over and land on your behind.

Celebrating my birthday on the summit of the mountain. It was one of the best birthdays ever.

2

3 Being part of such a great team of girls – the atmosphere was amazing.

2 Scotland's midges are annoying. The little biting insects love the area around Ben Nevis in the summer. I had a big red midge bite on my forehead, which wasn't great for my celebratory selfie!

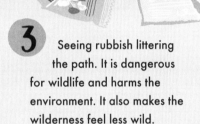

3 Seeing rubbish littering the path. It is dangerous for wildlife and harms the environment. It also makes the wilderness feel less wild.

EROSION AND LITTER

Ben Nevis is such a popular climb that the path has become very worn in places. It requires a lot of maintenance to keep it in good condition for walkers, so stay on the marked path to stop further erosion. The other major problem is litter. When you are hiking, remember to always take home anything you bring with you and don't leave litter or rubbish anywhere on the mountain.

WINTER OR SUMMER?

A winter hike up Ben Nevis is very different to a summer climb. Snow, ice and fog change the conditions completely and make any route dangerous if you don't know what you are doing. The north face of Ben Nevis is also a world-renowned ice climbing experience. It will test your route-finding, axe and crampon work, and belaying skills. Always go with a professional guide who can make sure you enjoy the adventure safely.

WILD ADVENTURES

If you don't have the mountains on your doorstep, there are plenty of other ways to test your mountaineering skills or experience the adrenaline rush of climbing.

1 Master MAP READING and Navigation

You will never regret learning to read a map and use a compass. Both take time and patience and it is best to build up your knowledge gradually. Why not start by finding a map of your local area and choosing a route to a landmark? No phones allowed! If you really enjoy it, join an orienteering group to sharpen your skills.

2 ABSEILING

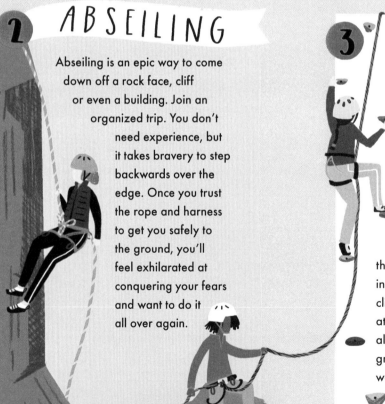

Abseiling is an epic way to come down off a rock face, cliff or even a building. Join an organized trip. You don't need experience, but it takes bravery to step backwards over the edge. Once you trust the rope and harness to get you safely to the ground, you'll feel exhilarated at conquering your fears and want to do it all over again.

3 ROCK CLIMBING

Rock climbing tests you physically and mentally. You have to be able to plot a route up a vertical rock face and then use power, flexibility and agility to reach the top. The amount of leg and forearm strength that climbing requires always amazes me. Oh, and you need a fair bit of nerve – you have to trust that you can reach that bump in the rock or that your toes will wedge into a crack. The most popular type of climbing is sport climbing, where you are attached by a rope to the rock face and also to your partner, or belayer, on the ground. Try your skills on an indoor wall first.

4 BOULDERING

Bouldering is climbing without a rope or harnesses. Try it on indoor walls with colour-coded routes or on freestanding boulders outdoors. The general rule is that you should be able to jump from the top and land safely. It's not easier just because you're closer to the ground. Bouldering is about problem solving: you have to be able to find a route as you go, trusting yourself to find hand and foot holds with no harness. If you slip there's nothing to break your fall.

5 Weaselling

Weaselling is fantastic fun: it's a cross between caving and gorge scrambling. You also don't need a head for heights, as rather than climbing upwards, you scramble, or "weasel" your way through small gaps between rocks and boulders. To get between rocks you might try rock-hopping, which is where you jump from boulder to boulder. It's a great way to build up your confidence and even more fun done as a team.

WHERE to go WILD

Langdale, England
Epic views, epic climbs and you can't move for climbing experts.

Snowdonia National Park, Wales
Try climbing, abseiling and even zip-lining through underground caverns.

Joshua Tree National Park, USA
There are thousands of boulder problems and climbing routes for all abilities.

Railay Beach, Thailand
Rock climb over the glittering ocean in this stunning beach spot.

WHERE TO CLIMB

There are indoor climbing walls in the most unlikely places. Inside abandoned churches and warehouses on industrial estates you will find walls that offer something for everyone. Loads of these places have taster sessions. Don't be scared, and remember everyone started somewhere. Lots of city parks also have climbing walls or boulders. Having got stuck bouldering in quite a few parks, I'd recommend always having someone to spot you on the way up and help you down.

EXTREMELY WILD ADVENTURES

Got a head for heights? Try these mountain adventures – the fresh mountain air will leave you feeling on top of the world.

1 PRACTISE with a PEAK

The first time you climb a mountain, start with something small and go on a good day in the summer. Test your kit. Get used to wearing a rucksack. And practise your navigation skills to see if this is the adventure for you. Two of my favourite walks are Striding Edge in the Lake District and High Cup Nick on the Pennine Way. Both are challenging, but have clearly marked paths so don't require masses of navigation.

FELL RUNNING in the LAKE DISTRICT
– Helen's Report –

I've only tried fell running once: in the Lake District with a guide. Going up was tough. I mean lung-burning, thigh-throbbing, stomach-churningly tough. I confess I had a few stops: I was doubled-over gasping for air. I honestly thought I might be sick, but I was in the zone, so on I went. Getting to the top didn't even feel like an achievement because there was no time to take in the view before turning round and hurtling back down. This is where I needed nerves of steel. The descent was so steep my legs felt as if they were moving independently of my body. I had my arms out wide to steady myself because the ground was slippery and uneven. My legs were going faster than my body and I lost my balance. Even though I knew it was going to happen, I could not stop myself from falling. My legs flew from underneath me, my bum hit the ground and down I slipped. You know when you fall and it hurts so much you can't speak otherwise you might cry? Well, that is how sore my bum was. I bit my tongue, held my breath and waited for some feeling to return to my butt cheeks. Needless to say, I slowed down a little bit for the last part of the descent!

2 FELL Running

Fell runners are hard-core. Running up and down hills in all weathers on all types of terrain is not for the faint-hearted. I used to watch in awe at the fell runners taking on the peaks at Windermere, Grasmere and Keswick in the Lake District. One minute they were in front of us on the field warming up. The next they were tiny dots, like ants, scurrying across the fells on the horizon. As they came back down the mountains, they would be covered in mud, sweat and even blood from where they'd fallen over.

WARNING

Adult supervision required for adventures.

3 MOUNTAIN BIKING

Mountain biking involves rough terrain and steep descents, so good suspension on your bike and thick tyres are essential. If I had a pound for every time I have flown over the handlebars of a mountain bike, I would be a rich lady. ALWAYS wear a helmet. And the minute you hesitate you will fall. The trick is to get back on after you have fallen. When you master a route by facing your fears and conquering them, you will be buzzing. All the mountain bikers I have met have one thing in common: they thrive on the rush of adrenaline they get from thundering down steep mountainsides peppered with obstacles, twists and turns. Dan Hanebrink, who designed my bike for the South Pole, was one of those guys.

WILD GIRL WISH LIST

The Bob Graham Round is an infamously tough fell-running challenge. The 66-mile circuit of 42 of the highest peaks in the Lake District has to be completed within 24 hours. Just writing that blows my mind. I have so much respect for anyone who has even attempted it. One day I hope to give it a go myself.

WHERE to go WILD

Gisburn Forest, England
One of my favourite mountain-biking spots.

Fairfax, USA
Amazing mountain biking and plenty of stunning peaks to hike.

Geirangerfjord, Norway
Unbeatable views on both foot or bike.

97

WILD GIRL Wall of Fame

These women have all reached inspirational heights.

Alison Hargreaves

In 1995, Alison Hargreaves became the first woman in history to summit the world's highest peak, Mount Everest, alone and without bottled oxygen or the support of a Sherpa team. Three months later, she died climbing K2 in Pakistan, the world's second-highest peak.

KAREN DRAKE

Karen Drake is the first paraplegic woman to hand-cycle across the Himalayas and she has climbed the legendary El Capitan in Yosemite National Park, USA, as well as Europe's tallest mountain, Mont Blanc. She is a silver medal-winning Paralympic athlete too.

Sophia 2006

SOPHIA DANENBERG

Sophia became the first African-American and first black woman in the world to climb Mount Everest in 2006. Sophia suffered from bronchitis and frostbite on her cheeks in her two months to the summit.

YOU!

WHERE WILL YOUR NEXT ADVENTURE TAKE YOU?

Jasmin Paris

The British ultra-runner, Jasmin Paris, smashed records when she won the 268-mile Montane Spine Race. She is the first ever woman to win the race outright, and she beat the previous record by 12 hours! As a new mum, she had to express milk for her baby on the way.

Wasfia Nazreen is the first Bangladeshi to climb the Seven Summits (the tallest mountains on each continent). At the top of each mountain she took out the Bangladesh flag and a hula hoop – making her the first person to hula-hoop on all Seven Summits too!

Wasfia Nazreen

Ashima Shiraishi first started climbing on boulders in Central Park, New York, aged 6. By the time she was 14 she was tackling climbs so difficult that no other woman had completed them before her. A World Championship gold-medal winner, Ashima is now considered one of the best climbers in the world.

Ashima Shiraishi

ADVENTURES

Adventures don't have to take you to faraway places. The countryside is our natural playground and it is just waiting to be explored. You can build a den, go walking or cycling, or try one of my all-time favourite outdoor adventures: wild camping.

My ultimate countryside adventure was when I attempted part of the Royal Marines Commando training in Dartmoor National Park in Devon for the television programme *Blue Peter*. I joined Royal Marines recruits from the Okehampton base for the very final part of their training: a 30-mile speed march across the moors in a time limit of 8 hours, while carrying a 18kg backpack. If they completed the speed march, they would be awarded their green berets.

Royal Marines Commandos are tough. They are one of the world's most elite land and sea fighting troops, trained to face danger in all kinds of challenging environments. When I asked a former Marine how hard Commando training would be, he told me to think of the hardest thing I had ever done and double it. I heard many such stories in the run up to this challenge. To say I was intimidated from the start was an understatement – and in this case, my nerves nearly broke me.

Marching across Dartmoor National Park with my army pack reminded me of all the incredible outdoor spaces that are on our doorsteps: footpaths, forests, bridleways, old railway lines and canal tow paths. Vast areas of countryside are designated national parks, or owned by trusts and charities so we can enjoy them. There are working farms, windmills, castles or historic houses with stunning grounds. There are nature reserves looked after by groups of dedicated volunteers who want to share their passion for the natural landscape and wildlife. Pull on your walking boots and join them!

WILD WORLD

Dartmoor is a national park in Devon covering 368 square miles. Open moorlands, rocky outcrops, rushing rivers and ancient woodlands make it an epic and varied wilderness.

Adventures on DARTMOOR

CHALLENGE: To attempt the Royal Marines Commando 30-mile speed march, known as the yomp. I would have to carry 18kg of equipment and I had 8 hours to complete the challenge.

ROYAL MARINES COMMANDO TRAINING

The Royal Marines Commando training is one of the longest and most gruelling programmes in the world. The final part of their thirty-two-week training involves four Commando tests in the space of a week. If they complete the tests, the recruits are awarded their much sought-after green berets.

1 ### The ENDURANCE Course

The recruits work their way through 2 miles of tunnels, pools, streams, bogs and woods. They then run 4 miles back to camp where they have to achieve six out of ten in a shooting test. The time limit is 73 minutes.

2 ### The 9-Mile SPEED MARCH

The recruits have to complete this in 90 minutes while carrying their equipment and rifle.

3 ### The TARZAN ASSAULT Course

An aerial assault course made up of ropes that has to be completed by the recruits in 13 minutes while carrying their equipment and rifle.

DARTMOOR

MEANS OF TRANSPORT
Foot

DISTANCE
30 miles

TIME LIMIT
8 hours

WEATHER
Whatever Dartmoor throws at you

PACK WEIGHT
18kg

+ The 30-Mile MARCH

A march across Dartmoor, which the recruits have to complete in under 8 hours, while carrying their equipment and rifle.

THIS IS WHAT I WAS GOING TO BE DOING

TRAINING and PREPARATION

When the idea of attempting the Royal Marines Commando speed march for television was suggested, I was keen to have a go, although I was nervous about how tough it was going to be. When I undertook the challenge in 2013, only a few female army officers had successfully completed the Commando course in the previous ten years. It wasn't until 2018 that women in the UK were allowed to serve in all military roles, including the Royal Marines and the SAS.

Commando training is a long, intense process designed to push the recruits to their mental and physical limits. The training lasts for thirty-two weeks, and the recruits build up their strength and stamina, and get used to carrying their heavy equipment. The final week involves four Commando tests, before the recruits are awarded their green berets and become Marines.

I was very aware that I was only dipping in to the recruits' training programme, and I made a basic mistake. I should have trained with the kit I would be carrying with me on the march. I wore my military-issue boots to break them in, but I should also have spent as much time as possible getting used to the 18kg backpack. This was the challenge where I was the least prepared in terms of my training – and it was going to show.

YOMP TASTER

To give me an idea of what was in store on the yomp, the senior staff at the Commando Training Centre in Devon agreed to show me the route of the 30-mile course. I tagged along with a group of recruits who were doing their march for real, so I was told to run on ahead. I wasn't wearing the heavy pack, so the 30 miles were tiring but relatively easy.

ENDURANCE TEST

Before I was allowed to attempt the yomp, I had to complete the endurance test under a time limit at the Commando Training Centre in Devon. On a cold day in driving rain, I jogged, sprinted and squelched my way around the assault course. I thought I was fit until I attempted it, but running up hills, jumping in and out of freezing pools, and crawling over ramps was exhausting.

Part of the course was the "sheep dip", a submerged tunnel I had to swim through. I had to dunk myself under the water, shut my eyes and kick until I came out the other side. It doesn't sound scary, but I couldn't see where I was going and there were twigs and leaves floating in the water. I'm glad I did it, although I wouldn't like to repeat it in a hurry.

I then had to run 4 miles back to base. I hadn't thought about the time limit until the last few hundred metres, and luckily I crossed the line in a time acceptable enough for the Marines to let me have a go at the speed march. What was I letting myself in for?

Dare I say fun? It was a cold, misty morning. Dartmoor looked epic. The officer in charge and I raced ahead and we could see the recruits behind us. In my head, I pretended it was a game. The recruits were chasing me and I was trying to evade capture. There was no pressure on me and no expectation – I wasn't even expected to do the full 30 miles, but we kept going because I was having fun. I finished that day confident I could take on the actual challenge.

KIT LIST

Part of the challenge of the yomp was being able to cover the distance while carrying heavy kit. Every recruit had the same items in their pack.

BOOTS

Heavy-duty black military-issue boots helped with grip on the uneven and wet terrain.

PACK

Inside the pack was safety equipment, medical supplies, waterproof clothes, GPS equipment, food rations and a survival kit.

FOOD

spaghetti

First Aid

MILITARY-ISSUE UNIFORM

The thick khaki military-issue uniform was hardwearing, but uncomfortable.

WATER

I had water bottles in my pack and there were also water stops on the course.

FOOD

There were stops en route: a banana break and a pasty stop. Because you're racing the clock, it's a grab and go scenario. I also took some Jelly Babies with me.

Jelly Babies

After the endurance test, I left the Commando Training Centre and went back to my normal life. I was walking the dog in my military-issue boots, thinking that would get me in shape for the yomp. Meanwhile, the recruits were in the middle of some of the hardest military training in the world.

When I returned to the Commando Training Centre to attempt the march for real, I was in for a shock. I spent a day watching the recruits complete some of their final Commando tests. I saw them successfully complete complicated courses on high ropes. They were close to the finish line, at the end of thirty-two weeks of brutal training and they were incredibly focused. They towered over me in height and they all had heavy-set shoulders and big muscles. I felt suddenly unprepared and out of my depth. My confidence hit the floor.

THE BACKPACK

I literally hit the floor when I first tried on the backpack I would be carrying. It was so heavy that when I put it on, I could barely stand up. How the heck was I supposed to march for 30 miles carrying this weight and complete the yomp within the time limit? If I'm honest, I wanted to sit down and say: "No way. I'm not doing this." But I couldn't. The Royal Marine staff at the Commando Training Centre had gone out of their way to accommodate me and make this happen. I couldn't let everyone down.

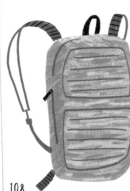

I can't tell you why I wasn't able to give myself a talking to and attack the challenge with confidence. I knew from my other adventures that physical strength wasn't everything. However, I couldn't shake the nerves: I was convinced that this time I had bitten off more than I could chew and that I was going to fail. I tried to put a brave face on in front of everyone but inside my stomach was in knots. I went to bed that night feeling sick, scared and alone.

NERVOUS NIGHT

I spent the night in the barracks. Someone stood outside the showers and bathroom when I went in because there wasn't a designated girls' loo. As I tried to sleep, all I could think of was how in the morning I would be setting off with a group of young men who had bonded together over a period of months. They had all been pushed to the limit and come out the other side as a team. All they had to do now was finish as a group within the 8-hour time limit. This was the final challenge before they officially became Marines. I was the untested outsider, dropped into their group. I was so aware of what was at stake. I didn't want to be at the back slowing them down.

The MARCH

Before facing the Dartmoor wilderness we were given a huge cooked breakfast. It felt a bit like being in a school canteen, only it was dark, cold and pretty much the middle of the night. Everyone looked like they knew what they were doing. I felt like the new kid at school. I was too scared to talk to anyone, which is not like me.

Out on the windy moors, we were put into our groups and set off at 10-minute intervals. No one was talking: it was just head down and get on with it. The first section was along a track and the pace was quicker than I had expected. It didn't feel long before we stopped for our first banana break.

We then headed onto the most exposed part of the moor. There were no tracks or buildings, just bogs and windswept grass. It was drizzling so it was chilly and there was no chance of seeing the sunrise through the fog. The marching became pretty challenging at this point. The recruits were powering through the boggy ground, making it look easy. I felt like I was moving through quicksand. I tried to go around the wetter patches, rather than waste energy going through them. The long grass slowed me down too.

WILD WORLD
DARTMOOR PONIES

Herds of hardy Dartmoor ponies thrive despite the poor vegetation and harsh weather conditions. Ponies have been on Dartmoor for a long time: hoof prints found on an archaeological dig were around 3,500 years old!

AT THE BACK

Soon I was at the back. I was desperately trying to maintain the pace so I didn't lose the group in the fog. By the time we reached the next section of road, I was almost jogging to keep up. In a car park we stopped for pasties, water and more bananas. I didn't feel like eating, but knew I had to. All I wanted to do was keep moving.

Parts of the route were beautiful: there was a section where the path was framed by tall trees and I could smell the damp forest. I loved seeing the Dartmoor ponies. However, the ground was really bumpy and when I stumbled, the weight of the pack meant it took me a bit of time to right myself again. I felt like a tortoise who had been given a shell that was intended for someone much bigger and broader.

As we chalked up the miles, the group started to talk more. Overall the recruits were on good form: some were finding it easy but others were struggling. Mentally I was finding it tough and there were real highs and lows. Every time I couldn't keep up with the pace, I thought I would have to pull out. Then there would be a section where I felt OK again and I thought I might actually be able to finish.

I was grateful that for the entire march I was accompanied by Physical Training Instructor CSgt Warren Keays-Smith. His support helped me immensely when I was struggling. I could tell he found the yomp a total breeze. In fact, he was carrying extra weight to make it more of a challenge!

NEARLY BROKEN

Fourteen miles into the challenge, I felt good. I even thought I might just finish within the time limit. At 16 miles, I hit a wall. I felt sick and I started to panic as the group moved further and further away from me.

BREAKING POINT

In the fog, I felt that I was miles behind, even though it was probably only a few hundred metres. I was desperate to complete the march within the time limit. I also didn't want to hold my group back. I really felt the pressure.

I needed to avoid pushing myself to the point where I would physically collapse and have to quit. Each mile was getting harder. I kept saying to CSgt Keays-Smith, "I have to do it, I have to do it!" At 16 miles, I knew I just wasn't going to make it with my group. The weight on my back was making every step harder and harder. I was given the option to hand in my backpack and continue the march without it. It was an agonizing decision, but in the end I gave in.

As the pack was removed, I felt like a mental and physical weight had been lifted from me. I now knew I could finish the march within the time limit. I stopped panicking and started enjoying myself. I dished out Jelly Babies and chatted with the recruits who wanted distracting. The challenge no longer felt impossible. Instead, the end was in sight.

TEAM SPIRIT

When I was struggling, my group offered to carry my pack for me. They promised to give it back to me at the end, so it would look like I had carried it the whole way round. They weren't trying to show off. They genuinely wanted everyone in our group to finish together and in one piece. I couldn't believe how selfless the offer was. However, I didn't want to fib and pretend I had completed the yomp under the full conditions. That would undermine the recruits' remarkable achievements. I treasure their offer to this day – it was one of the kindest things I have experienced. I had been so intimidated by my group when we first set off. By the time we crossed the finish line, within the time limit, I was in awe of the ability and attitude of the Marines.

TOUGH CHOICES

To this day, I regret the decision to hand in the backpack. In the moment, I decided that it was more important to keep up with the group than it was to carry the pack. But I don't like the fact I didn't complete the full challenge. With hindsight I know where I went wrong. I normally train as hard as I possibly can for adventures, so that when I get to the start line, I know deep down I have done more than I need to. That gives me confidence. On this occasion I shuffled to the yomp start line feeling like I had not trained hard enough. I doubted myself, and I think that is why I gave up the pack. I convinced myself I couldn't do it. When I look back, did I give it everything? No. I don't think I did. I should have pushed myself a bit further. This was the adventure I let my nerves and insecurities get the better of me.

Adventure REPORT

BEST BITS

1 The team spirit. The camaraderie in my group was so inspiring.

I learned two things on this adventure. The most important one applies to life: never judge people before you know them. At the beginning, I was intimidated by the Marines. I thought they would leave me to tackle the yomp alone. By the end I discovered that they were not only strong, they were selfless too.

I also learned a priceless lesson about taking control of your mind. When I saw my group on the start line, I compared myself to them and began to doubt myself. I convinced myself I was physically incapable of the challenge. If I had told myself I could do it, that it was well within my abilities, maybe this adventure would have had a different end. Especially as I loved the second half without the pack. The tough weather conditions and the uneven ground were experiences I embraced. I should have had the same can-do attitude to my pack at the start.

The Dartmoor landscape. It was otherworldly in the fog and crisp cold air. To be out there at first light was pretty special.

3 Watching the recruits get their green berets. They had completed world-renowned training and it was a total privilege to see them get their reward.

4 The hot shower after the yomp.

RESPECT

I cannot praise the recruits I marched with highly enough. They would have been well within their rights to have left me to my own devices. They did the opposite. They offered to help. They were willing to risk their chances of not finishing the yomp to help me. It was an unbelievable demonstration of team spirit that I will never forget. I will also never again drive past a sign for Dartmoor without feeling sick with nerves.

FAILURE IS AN OPTION

I love adventures that people think are impossible. And I also believe that it's OK to have a go at something and fail. How boring would life be if everything was plain sailing? There's no celebration or triumph in achieving something that you always knew was going to be a walk in the park. Even though this adventure didn't end how I wanted, I will never regret taking on – and almost completing – the yomp.

WORST BITS

1 Letting that backpack get the better of me. I wish I had done the full 30 miles with the pack.

2 The military-issue trousers. The rough fabric made my legs so sore, if anything touched them, it felt as if my skin had been burned.

3 Falling behind the group. Every time the group moved in front of me I panicked and wasted energy worrying.

WILD ADVENTURES

There are so many different places in the countryside to have all sorts of adventures. What are you waiting for? Get out there and go exploring.

1 BUILD a WOODLAND DEN

Look for dry fallen branches on a forest floor to create an A-shaped framework, supported by a longer branch. Never break living branches off trees. Leave an opening in your framework to serve as your entrance and exit. Then gather as many fallen small sticks and twigs as you can to fill in the gaps between the branches. The fewer gaps in your structure, the warmer you will be.

2 VISIT a FARM

Visit a farm and discover more about feeding and grooming animals and growing crops. If you time your visit right, you might be able to help with bottle-feeding newly born lambs.

3 EXPLORE A NATIONAL PARK

If you love wide open skies, wildlife, vast forests, ancient monuments and historic castles, why not visit a national park? These special protected places are packed with different types of adventures: whether it is walking, cycling, boating, climbing or wildlife-watching.

4 Go on a Cycling Adventure

You can't talk about exploring the countryside without mentioning bikes. I've mentioned mountain biking elsewhere, and I also love long cycle rides with friends. You don't have to go on busy roads: there are tracks, bridleways and tiny lanes that will allow you to weave your way across the countryside or through national parks at your own pace. Just don't forget your picnic! And if you want to make new friends, why not sign up for an organized group cycle ride?

OO-MILE CYCLE RIDE
– Helen's Report –

Cycling doesn't have to be about speed. I must have been the slowest rider on the Manchester 100. There were just too many people to chat to, and cycling those hundred miles I had the time of my life. I loved cycling from London to Brighton too. Just before you reach Brighton, you have to cycle up a steep and winding hill called Ditchling Beacon. It requires a low gear and a lot of leg strength. It's worth it for the views, the pats on the back from your fellow cyclists and the ice-cream van at the top. And even better is relaxing on Brighton Beach with fish and chips at the end of the ride.

5 GO Camping

Camping is one of my all-time favourite things. I think I sleep better in a tent than I do in my own bed. There is something so invigorating about sleeping under canvas after a day out and about in the fresh air. With your family, decide on a campsite (most will have toilets and washing facilities) and pitch your tent. If there isn't a campsite nearby, you can always start in your back garden. If the campsite allows it, ask an adult to help you make a camp fire.

WHERE to go WILD

Visit any and all of these incredible national parks across the UK.

Brecon Beacons
The Broads
Cairngorms
Dartmoor
Exmoor
Lake District
Loch Lomond & The Trossachs
New Forest
Northumberland
North York Moors
Peak District
Pembrokeshire Coast
Snowdonia
South Downs
Yorkshire Dales

WARNING
Adult supervision required for adventures.

6 Try STAR GAZING

On a warm, clear night, away from the light pollution of a town or city, take a moment to sit back and look up at the moon and stars. If you are lucky, you might see a shooting star or meteor.

EXTREMELY WILD ADVENTURES

Want to take your countryside adventures to the next level? These extremely wild adventures are for you!

1 GO WILD CAMPING

This means going off the beaten track and camping away from a designated campsite. You could also try bivvying, which is when you put your sleeping bag in a waterproof cover and sleep outside. It is worth it to have the wilderness to yourself. Make sure camping is allowed wherever you go. Remember to tread lightly: take all your rubbish with you, and stay on the marked paths where possible to protect plants and animals and stop erosion. Don't pick living things or disturb wildlife.

2 Sleep in a BOTHY or MOUNTAIN Hut

There are dozens of small huts, called bothies, in some of the most beautiful parts of the countryside that are open and free for anybody to stay in. Don't expect luxury: most don't have beds or toilets. You could end up sharing with a few strangers and you must remember to follow the Bothy Code. It's a unique way to sleep in a remote area without having to carry a tent. A bothy or mountain hut can also give you shelter if the weather turns bad.

Embracing a life outdoors means you are at the mercy of the elements, and the weather won't always go your way. I was doing some cold-weather training in Iceland when things went badly wrong. The weather got nastier, harsher and colder than anyone had forecasted. It was dangerous to stay outdoors, so we had to abandon our plan. Luckily we weren't far from a mountain shelter. Even though no one had stayed in it for months, it was warm because it had geothermal water running through the water pipes. I remember curling up like a cat on the floor because it was so snug and welcoming after being battered by the weather. The experience was a good lesson in keeping an eye on the weather and planning for the worst. Always think about what you would do in the worse-case scenario.

3 FORAGE for your DINNER

Finding food in the wild for free is known as foraging. With all foraging you must have a trained adult with you who knows what to look for. The first rule is that you must never eat a wild plant or mushroom unless you are absolutely certain what it is. It could be deadly poisonous or a protected species. But you'll be amazed at the amount of food you can find outdoors. My favourite is wild garlic, which you can find in damp, shady woodlands. Pick young leaves from late March onwards. And I adore blackberries, which are easy to identify and plentiful in the autumn months. Eat them straight from the bush or take them home and freeze them. Remember not to go onto private land and don't pick too much. Avoid areas close to roads or where a dog may have gone to the toilet.

WHERE to go WILD

Kielder Forest, England
Sleep in a bothy in the middle of these epic woods. One of the best night's sleeps I've ever had!

Ordesa, Spanish Pyrenees
Beautiful mountain huts and wild camping.

Katmai National Park, USA
Camp out but be alert for bears!

WILD GIRL Wall of Fame

These women have all had exciting countryside adventures.

PHILIPPA TATTERSALL

Captain Philippa "Pip" Tattersall made military history in 2002 by becoming the first woman to complete the Royal Marine Commando training and win a green beret. After successfully completing the 30-mile yomp, she conquered the Tarzan Assault Course on her third attempt.

Hannah Engelkamp trekked 1,000 miles around the circumference of Wales with a headstrong donkey named Chico. They followed a footpath around the edge of Wales, wild camping or sleeping in tipis, yurts and hay barns. They arrived back where they started six months later, with only a few creative detours when Chico couldn't climb over a stile.

Hannah ENGELKAMP

ANNIE Londonderry

In 1895, Annie Londonderry – real name Annie Cohen Kopchovsky – became the first woman to cycle around the world. It is thought her nine-month journey was a wager. Although it's suspected that she may have travelled by ship and train as well as cycling, to travel 9,604 miles across the world as a solo woman at the time was no mean feat!

Mirna Valerio is on a mission to bring body positivity to the world of endurance running. When she started training for her first marathon, she set up her blog Fat Girl Running. Since then, Mirna has become an inspirational adventurer, trail runner and ultra-marathon racer.

MIRNA VALERIO

ANNA McNUFF

Anna McNuff is an all-round epic human. Her adventures include: cycling 11,000 miles through every state in America; running New Zealand's 1,911 mile-long Te Araroa trail; cycling the spine of the Andes, the largest mountain range in the world; and roller-blading 100 miles around Amsterdam. Anna also has pink hair and never sees the sky as the limit. (Girl crush alert!)

Mira Rai grew up in a remote Nepalese village. Aged 14, she took part in what she thought was a training run, only to discover that she had accidentally entered and won a race. Mira is now a record-beating trail and sky runner, and wants to inspire other girls to follow her path.

Mira Rai

INSERT PHOTO HERE

YOU!

WHERE WILL YOUR NEXT ADVENTURE TAKE YOU?

A field or a fell aren't the only places to have an adventure. Sometimes all you need to do is look at a familiar place in a different way. A city might seem far away from a mountain wilderness, but there are adventures waiting if you know where to look. And remember, just being out of your comfort zone is an adventure in itself.

It is easy to think that cities are just a maze of concrete pavements, tall buildings and busy roads. However, that doesn't take into consideration how exciting the sights and smells of a new city can be. Mumbai in India is one of the loudest, in-your-face places I have ever been. But I loved it because it was the complete opposite of everything I was used to. Dhaka in Bangladesh is the same: around every corner is something surprising. There are crumbling buildings stacked on top of each other, street vendors selling all kinds of brightly coloured items, and people hanging out of the windows of cars as they whizz along at lightning speed. Everything is so different and intriguing, it is impossible not to have an adventure exploring the streets.

And that's the cities themselves. Sometimes travelling to your destination is half the fun. Whether it's a red bus in London, a tram in Lisbon, a tuk tuk in Mumbai or a yellow New York taxi, travelling like a local is a great way to experience a new city.

Even familiar cities can be transformed into adventures if you are prepared to try something new. I was lucky enough to see London differently when, for charity, I was filmed walking a 150-metre-long high wire. I had to walk between the towers of Battersea Power Station, on the banks of the River Thames. I can safely say that it is a building I have never looked at in the same way since.

WILD WORLD

Flowing through London, the River Thames is slowly recovering from the damage pollution caused to the water quality. The river is now home to 125 species of fish. Mammals such as seals, porpoises and even a whale have been spotted swimming in its waters.

Adventures on the HIGH WIRE

CHALLENGE: To walk a 150-metre high wire stretched between two of the towers of Battersea Power Station. I would be 66 metres above the ground.

SOUTH WEST LONDON

Pimlico
Kennington
Vauxhall
Chelsea
RIVER THAMES

LONDON

LOCATION
Battersea Power Station, London

HEIGHT OF WIRE
66 metres

LENGTH OF WIRE
150 metres

WEATHER
Windy and drizzly

My Trip in NUMBERS

18mm
width of wire (about the width of a 10p piece)

3
months training

12kg
balance pole weight

8
metre balance pole

11
minutes to complete the walk

MY INSPIRATION FROM UP HIGH

I didn't find school that easy, but I worked hard and putting in the effort ultimately paid off. I guess that taught me that anything is in your grasp if you are prepared to work for it. So rather than being put off by a challenge that looks impossible, I often think, "Why can't I do that?" That's exactly what I felt after I watched the documentary *Man on Wire*. In 1974, Philippe Petit walked a high wire between the twin towers of New York's World Trade Center, 400 metres above the ground, without a safety net. I was completely gripped by the daring nature of his challenge. Inspired by his bravery and skill, I wanted to attempt my own wire-walking feat.

TRAINING and PREPARATION

Once I had decided to attempt a wire walk, all kinds of suggestions were made for where I could do it: Victoria Falls in Africa, or closer to home at Wembley Stadium in London. The towers at the then disused Battersea Power Station were eventually chosen. All the complicated logistics for the challenge were out of my hands. I had the small task of learning how to walk on a wire, and my training began at circus school.

CIRCUS SCHOOL

Circus school was full of incredible flexible performers dangling on silks suspended from the ceiling, bending themselves through hoops or dancing across wires. I was intimidated: I had never done gymnastics before and I am far from bendy.

To begin with I wasn't even allowed on a wire. I had to take three paces along a line on the floor while holding my arms in the air for balance. I needed to learn to keep my head up and the muscles in my stomach, back and bum tight.

I progressed to walking across a wire just a few centimetres from the floor. Eventually, I was allowed to try a wire 30cm from the floor, then a few metres. There was always a pile of crash mats underneath the wire, so I wouldn't hurt myself when I fell. And I fell a lot. Most of my attempts ended after two or three paces. Sometimes I couldn't even manage those few steps without crashing to the ground. It was mortifying. I would love to tell you there was a magic moment and something clicked, but it didn't. I just had to keep getting back on the wire and trying. Again and again. Because I knew practice was the only thing that could possibly get me across a wire at Battersea Power Station.

MY FIRST PERFORMANCE

My first challenge was to complete a wire walk in front of an audience at the circus. I fell off three times before I made it across. I was wearing a ridiculous costume and I felt like a fool, especially as the audience kept laughing. Stiff with nerves and embarrassment, I took a few deep breaths. I told myself I couldn't let my nerves get the better of me. I picked myself up and finished walking the wire. It wasn't my finest hour and certainly not the adrenaline-inducing high I was hoping would build my confidence.

FOCUSING IN FRANCE

Jade Kindar-Martin and Karine Mauffrey then taught me how to walk a high wire. They are perhaps the coolest couple I have ever met. Jade is a world-renowned wire-walker and Karine is a stuntwoman. They have a high wire across the garden of their home in the south of France. It was the perfect, if not slightly intense, place to learn.

Jade made me stand still on the wire, holding the long balance pole that wire-walkers use to stabilize themselves. He wanted to improve my focus, so he encouraged me only to think about my next three steps. There are usually a million things going through my mind. Standing in silence, thinking only about the wire, was hard. I stood on that wire no matter what the weather was like: I even practised in the snow.

I didn't realize how fit you have to be to walk on a wire, but the balance pole is heavy and holding it steady requires a lot of arm and back strength. Karine took me running to build my fitness. We also hiked up into the hills near their house carrying rocks to build up my arm strength.

FEAR OF FALLING

A lot of people imagine that the wire is flexible and bendy. It isn't: it's stretched so tightly that it is more like a solid beam. I would carefully slide one foot over the top of the other to keep as much contact with the wire as possible. It wasn't easy and I fell onto the wire almost every time I attempted a few steps.

Thankfully, Jade had rigged the wire with a harness and safety wire. When I slipped or lost my balance, my body would hit the wire and then the safety wire would click in, leaving me bouncing around like a puppet on a string. The harness and safety wire stopped me from hitting the ground countless times. It was embarrassing, but it saved me from a broken leg or two.

However, believe me when I say there is no polite way to describe the pain of landing on a wire. You can't break your fall, because you are holding on to the balance pole. Most of the time your body takes the full impact of the wire and it feels like landing on a metal bar. At times my bum was so black and blue it was too painful to sit on a bike. My arms were also badly bruised from pulling myself back up onto the wire after a fall. Arnica cream, which helps reduce swelling, became my best friend.

MENTAL STRENGTH

Training for the wire was tough mentally as well as physically. A lot of it was about confidence and I had to believe that I could do it. When I was nervous, my breathing became quick and shallow and it made my body tremble. This would make the wire shake underneath my feet and I would worry about losing my balance. I found that the moment I questioned myself, I would wobble, and once I wobbled it was almost impossible to avoid falling off. I learned that the only way to deal with the situation was to blow out everything I was keeping knotted up inside me: tension in my muscles and tightness in my chest. By controlling my breathing and blowing the nerves away I was able to master the situation. Gradually I stopped wobbling and started walking.

YOGA AND PILATES

I find it hard to concentrate and stay focused. For wire-walking you need to be able to block everything out and stay calm and in control. I used hot yoga and Pilates sessions as a way to train both my mind and body. Breathing exercises helped me too. Try this one to help you clear your mind: close one nostril with your thumb and inhale. Then move your thumb to the other nostril and exhale. Sometimes it's good to sit down and take a breath. Stillness is important.

WALKING THE WIRE

The wire I was practising on was 87 metres in length, stretching across a garden and stream. Over a month, I built up my distance. First, I went halfway across the wire. Then I walked backwards to my starting point. I learned how to turn on the wire by going up onto my tiptoes and pivoting around. The hardest bit was keeping control of the massive balance pole when I turned in the air.

Metre by metre I built the distance up until I could walk the full length of the wire, turn around and walk back. Jade even taught me to do a salute and sit down on the wire – both of which were bruising experiences. I knew that I was now close to the real distance of 150 metres I would be walking, and in that walk I wouldn't have to do a turn. I told myself that if I could do this distance with the turn, surely I could walk the wire at Battersea Power Station.

KIT LIST

You don't need much kit to walk a wire. What you do have will help save you from serious injury.

BALANCE POLE

Long, heavy and awkward, the balance pole was an essential piece of kit for helping me maintain my balance. It also made it easier for people to spot me in the sky!

CYCLING SHORTS

The padding in cycling shorts was essential protection from the worst of the bruising. I wore two pairs at a time.

ARNICA CREAM

Arnica helped bring down my bruises.

ARNICA
Cream

SAFETY HARNESS

I wore a safety harness when on the high wire. It clipped on to a safety wire above my head. If I lost my footing the harness and wire would stop me falling. It wasn't comfortable and it added to my bruises, but it saved me from breaking my limbs.

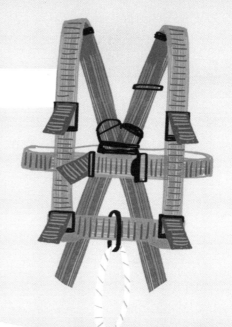

COSTUME

I was going to be exposed to the elements up on the wire. I decided on a red jacket that was eye-catching but would also keep me warm.

WIRE-WALKING SHOES

I had special shoes with suede soles that moulded to the wire underneath my feet. They had tight laces that criss-crossed over my feet so each step was as controlled as possible.

MY HIGH WIRE DIARY

The day of my high-wire walk between the towers of Battersea Power Station dawned wet, windy and cold. It was a day you wouldn't really want to spend outside, let alone walk across a wire suspended in the sky. I was so nervous that I thought I was going to throw up.

When I was getting ready at the television studio, I asked the make-up artist to put lots of make-up on me and give me an elaborate hairdo. I wanted to give myself a confidence boost and I thought dressing up for the occasion would help. I took a taxi to Battersea Power Station. At that time the massive building was disused and derelict. As we approached I could just about see the wire. It was a faint line in the sky, strung between the huge white towers.

FEAR OF THE UNKNOWN

Even from that distance, I could see the wire dipped in the middle. I had only ever walked a straight wire, never one that dipped. I was going to have to walk down the wire and then back up again. The knot in my stomach got tighter. When we got to Battersea, I asked the production team why the wire was dipping. I was told that if the wire was straight, the tension might pull the towers down. Having a dip eased the pressure. This wasn't exactly reassuring. Microphones and harnesses were attached to me and cameras were shoved in my face. "How do you feel?" everyone kept asking me. The truth is I was so afraid, I could barely speak.

THE CLIMB UP

I had asked my parents and some friends to come and watch, and I felt awful for them. It wasn't going to be a fun experience either for them or for me. The old power station was a daunting environment. There were dead birds lying around and a rat scurried away from me. A cold wind was blowing off the river and a train or two thundered by. I had practised with Jade in France in a lovely garden. I didn't feel prepared for this: I was scared and intimidated.

The wire was supported by a scaffolding framework. Climbing slowly up the ladders to the platform at the top was nerve-racking. Drizzle was blowing in my face. Tense conversations were crackling through the production team's walkie-talkies as they debated if I could begin. I waited on a metal platform, no bigger than a tea tray, holding the balance pole in my frozen fingers.

Jade told me to remember what he had taught me, but by this point my mind was totally blank. Being clipped into the harness and safety line seemed to take for ever. "I just want to go," I said again and again. I needed to start before I lost my nerve completely. The wind picked up speed. I shifted my weight from foot to foot and looked out to the other tower. I watched the wire moving in the wind. In training, I had been used to the ground gradually falling away but this was different. It was a steep and definite drop, with knots of metal and debris on the ground beneath me. I searched the safety team's faces for the nod of approval. Finally it came.

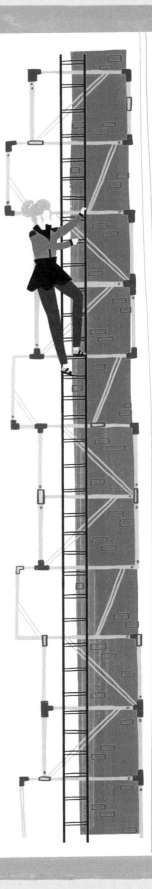

DANGER ZONE!
WEATHER

The production team were worried about the weather. If it was windy would I blow off the wire? If it was cold, would rain water freeze on the wire and make it too slippery? We had to make a decision about when it would be safe for me to set off. In the end the start was delayed by 40 minutes because of the high wind. That really didn't help my nerves.

I went for it and stepped out onto the wire. Immediately I knew I hadn't got my balance quite right so I stepped back onto the platform. I took a breath and tried again. One. Two. Three. Just three steps at a time. One. Two. Three.

ON THE WIRE

My pace was quicker than in training, because the wire was sloping down into the dip and it was slippery. I looked a metre ahead and kept my focus on the wire. I took three paces, then another three. The safety line above my head kept catching and I had to jerk it forward. All I wanted was to get across and finish in one piece. I kept clenching my stomach and bum, trying to keep my core as solid as possible. As I came out of the dip and started to go upwards, the pole felt heavy and my arms and back were burning. I was so tense, I had to tell myself to keep breathing.

I was doing it. I was nailing it. I tried not to look up at the platform where I would finish: I knew I couldn't get too excited. Slowly, step by step, the platform got closer. I thought about doing the salute Jade had taught me or sitting down on the wire. However, I wasn't sure if I could do it in the wind and rain, with the wire wobbling more than any I had ever practised on.

DANGER ZONE!
FALLING OFF THE WIRE

Professional high-wire walkers don't wear harnesses. They train their entire lives to not need one and I'm in awe of their bravery. The safety harness I wore when walking the high wire was clipped to a safety wire running above my head. If I had fallen, the wire would have clicked in and broken my fall. The safety team told me not to expect a soft landing: the impact of the harness could break my ribs.

After 11 minutes the end was only metres away, but I had to keep focusing on my next three steps. The wind had made my eyes water and it was hard to see. I had this fear of stepping off the wire too soon and missing the last step onto the platform. Despite my blurry vision, I could see my friends waiting for me, holding their breath.

THE FINISH

Unlike any of my other adventures, I was desperate for this one to be over and to take that final step onto something solid. The 11 minutes felt like seconds. Planting my foot onto that platform was the most unbelievable feeling. Fireworks went off. My friends cheered. I wanted to hug someone but I had to hold the huge heavy pole. Instead I hopped from one foot to the other and jumped around. And if I'm honest, the moment I finished, I wished I could go back out and do it again. I was riding a wave of pure exhilaration and suddenly I felt invincible.

Adventure REPORT

I loved the rush of adrenaline I got when I stepped off the high wire. I had pushed myself to do something that I hadn't believed myself to be capable of when I started training. And I had learned the importance of emptying my mind and focusing on a single goal.

I will never forget the looks on my friends' faces as I set off to walk the high wire. They were trying so hard not to look frightened for me. One of my mates, Andy, grabbed me by the shoulders, looked me in the eye and told me to go out there and smash it. I felt a bit braver after that. When you are doubting yourself, good friends and kind words from the people you love will make you feel confident. I got the best hugs and high-fives afterwards, especially from my mum and dad.

STYLING IT OUT

Looking back I laugh at the costume and make-up I wore that day. Often high-wire walkers wear white. I didn't feel like I qualified as a real high-wire walker, so I didn't want to do that. Instead I went all out on an elaborate red and black costume. It made me feel like a dare-devil which gave me a much-needed confidence boost.

BEST BITS

1 Achieving something I genuinely thought was impossible.

2 The feeling of being high up above everyone and everything. I felt a bit like a superhero.

3 Learning to focus and concentrate on a single thing. I am rubbish at it in normal situations.

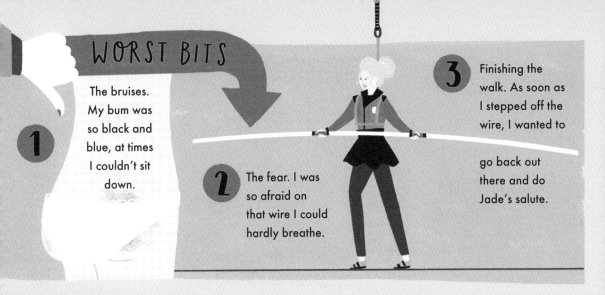

WORST BITS

1 The bruises. My bum was so black and blue, at times I couldn't sit down.

2 The fear. I was so afraid on that wire I could hardly breathe.

3 Finishing the walk. As soon as I stepped off the wire, I wanted to go back out there and do Jade's salute.

TEAMWORK

Walking the wire was tough and terrifying. However, the bigger challenge was being allowed to do it in the first place. It's impossible to talk about this adventure without acknowledging my colleagues and friends at the BBC who made it happen. Teamwork is vital to most ambitious adventures. Surround yourself with good people who believe in you and want to keep you safe. That might be your family, your friends, your teachers or your guide leader. Never underestimate how much those around you will inspire you to take on new things. And when you can share success with them, it's the most amazing feeling.

137

WILD ADVENTURES

These adventures will give you a different perspective on a familiar city.

/////
WARNING
Adult supervision
required for adventures.

1 GO SLACKLINING

Slacklining is an excellent way to have fun in the park. Simply string the bouncy strap between two established trees, about knee height from the ground, jump on and try to stay there. Put your arms in the air for balance. Challenge your friends to a competition to find who can stay on the longest. Or, if you're in my family, throw soft balls at whoever is on the line to find out how well they can balance.

2 LEARN Circus SKILLS

You can learn many kinds of circus skills at schools and academies, all of which will improve your strength, coordination, balance and nerve. Test your head for heights with the trapeze or wire-walking. You can also try aerial hoops or aerial silks. Aerial hoop performers make it look easy, but when I tried it I discovered just how much strength and flexibility you need to look effortless in the air.

TUK TUK
mumbai

TRAIN-TOKYO

LONDON BUS

BIKE-AMSTERDAM

3 Try a Zip Wire

Whizzing through the air on a zip wire, watching the streets spin beneath you, is one of the most exciting city adventures you can have. Lots of cities have zip wires in parks, often combined with high-rope courses, where you can push your bravery to the limit.

4 GO UP HIGH

Going up high is a brilliant way to see a city from a different perspective. Look for city parks with hills or famous monuments, or towers and buildings that are open to the public to climb. Once you're up high, enjoy being at the top of a landmark that thousands of people look up at every day. How does the city skyline look different?

GO DOWN LOW

Going underground is another superb way to explore a city. Vaults, catacombs, abandoned stations or hidden rivers all lurk underneath the pavements of cities across the world. Going underground can be a creepy experience – even the sound of your breath will make you jump.

WHERE to go WILD

Your local gymnastics club or circus school
A great place to work on your balance and flexibility.

Zip Now, London
The world's longest urban zip wire.

Eiffel Tower, Paris
One of the world's most famous city towers.

The Vaults, Edinburgh
The atmosphere is so spooky!

CITY TRANSPORT ADVENTURES

Sometimes a journey through a city is an adventure in itself. Travel like a local in these cities:

Sydney FERRY

TAXI NEW YORK

EXTREMELY WILD ADVENTURES

Take a walk on the really wild side by trying these city adventures.

1 TRY a HIGH-Adrenaline SPORT

Boxing, kickboxing, wrestling, fencing, Judo – these are just a few of the high-adrenaline sports that will quite literally give you adventure kicks. Grappling with an opponent, fighting with a sword and landing punches in the ring all require a combination of strength, coordination and mental discipline. You will also be part of a community and that feeling of team spirit is unbeatable.

BOXING
– Helen's Report –

I tried boxing for the first time when I was asked to take part in a celebrity charity match. The scariest bit wasn't the fact I had to fight an opponent on television. It was stepping into a ring in front of the girls at the England Boxing camp to learn how to spar. I skipped around the ring, too scared to throw punches. "Hit her!" my coach Phil Sellers yelled. "Hit me!" Natasha, my opponent, urged. So I did. I didn't feel great about it. Until she caught me a few times, then I retaliated. In the weeks running up to my fight, I met women and girls who amazed me. They were committed and dedicated, spending hours training in the gym building their physical strength and mental resilience.

When I walked into the ring for my charity fight, my insides were in knots. Phil had told me to get out there and look like I meant business. I had to land the first punch and get in my opponent's face quickly. I respect and admire her, but I wanted to show her, the judges and the women I had trained with that I was confident and able. I went for it. I did everything Phil had told me and I was happy to retire after that one bout undefeated. I was still picking bloody scabs out of my nose the week after! I still box with Phil now and again – there is no better way to clear your head.

GO on a FOOD Adventure

When it comes to a food adventure, you have to abandon any idea of what you like and what you don't like. If you're somewhere new, the chances are you will never have tried what you're about to be offered. That can be a bit scary, but try to put your feelings aside and go for the new experience. There's usually a reason why people are so proud of their food, so take their word for it and get stuck in to local recommendations and delicacies. I've eaten guinea pig in Lima, Turkish delight in Istanbul and queued for hours for bagels in Montreal. Some of those things were more tasty than others, but all were unforgettable experiences in their own way.

TRY a HISTORICAL Re-enactment

This sounds a bit geeky, I know! But warriors with swords and deadly bows and arrows aren't nerdy. I went to Gladiator School in Rome and I loved it. I was dressed head-to-toe in warrior costume and was slaying the boys with my heavy iron sword. Look for re-enactment groups in your local town or city – ask at a museum.

WARNING
Adult supervision required for adventures.

WHERE to go WILD

Your local sports club or centre
Get advice about different sports or classes you could join.

Gladiator School, Rome
Embrace battle by finding your inner gladiator.

Grand Bazaar, Istanbul
This covered market has an incredible array of sights and smells.

WILD GIRL Wall of Fame

Be inspired by these women's high-adrenaline urban adventures.

KARINE MAUFFREY

Karine Mauffrey is a stuntwoman and circus artist. She has starred in Cirque du Soleil and been a stuntwoman on hit films. She married fellow Cirque du Soleil star Jade Kindar-Martin on a high wire stretched over the grounds of a château in France.

Nicola Adams started boxing when she accidentally joined a boxing class at her local gym. Now, not only is she a double Olympic gold medal winner, she is also the only female boxer in the history of the sport to have won every major title available to her: Olympic, World, European and Commonwealth.

NICOLA ADAMS
Boxing superstar wins

Luci 'STEEL' Romberg

Luci Romberg is the best female freerunner in the world and a professional stuntwoman. She describes freerunning as "urban gymnastics", and the world champion loves the confidence the sport gives her.

INSERT
PHOTO
HERE

YOU!

WHERE WILL YOUR NEXT
ADVENTURE TAKE YOU?

Atita Verghese

Atita Verghese is a skateboarder from Bangalore who started the online platform Girl Skate India. It connects female skaters with each other and allows Atita to organize classes, clinics and tours.

LILY RICE

Teenager Lily Rice is one of the best Wheelchair Motocross (WCMX) competitors in the world and the first female in Europe to achieve a wheelchair backflip (and only the second female in the world). She won a silver medal at the 2018 World WCMX Championships.

Claire Lomas

Claire Lomas, who was paralysed from the waist down in an accident, became the first paralysed person to walk the London Marathon. In 2012, she completed the 26.2 miles in 17 days wearing a robotic suit. She continues to take on mind-blowing challenges for charity.

For my mum. Ever since I saw you try to skateboard,
I have believed that girls can do anything.
H.S.

For three generations of inspiring women,
Grandma, Mum & Sydney.
L.K.

ACKNOWLEDGEMENTS

Many of the adventures and trips I have written about were done when I made programmes for and with the BBC. Although I ended up on television, those trips were team events. I will be for ever in awe of and grateful to my colleagues and friends who coaxed me through some dark times – and took amazing photos.

Special thanks to: BBC Children's Television; *Blue Peter*; Sports Relief; the Royal Marines; British Canoeing and Mark Hoile; Rory Coleman; Jade and Karine Kindar-Martin; Conrad Dickinson; Sarah McNair-Landry and Niklas Norman.

First published 2019 by Walker Books Ltd
87 Vauxhall Walk, London SE11 5HJ

10 9 8 7 6 5 4 3 2 1

Text © 2019 Helen Skelton
Illustrations © 2019 Liz Kay

The right of Helen Skelton and Liz Kay to be identified as author and illustrator respectively of this work has been asserted by them in accordance with the Copyright, Designs and Patents Act 1988.

This book has been typeset in Futura and Toolbox Mustache

Printed in Italy

British Library Cataloguing in Publication Data: a catalogue record for this book is available from the British Library.

ISBN 978-1-4063-8764-3

www.walker.co.uk

PHOTO CREDITS

All reasonable efforts have been made by the author and publishers to trace the copyright owners of the images reproduced in this book. In the event that the author or publishers are notified of any mistakes or omissions by copyright owners after publication of this book, the author and publisher will endeavour to rectify the position accordingly for any subsequent printing.

All photos © Helen Skelton except:
Mike Carling © pages 6 (left), 10, 22
Roland Winkler © pages 6 (right), 14, 17, 19
Richard Turley © page 27
Eric McFarland © pages 30 (bottom), 32, 45 (bottom), 63, 67, 68
Kieron Schiff © page 39, 45 (top)
Pixabay © page 42, 111
Nigel Bradley © page 46
Stuart Dunn © pages 54, 57 (left), 64, 73
Lucy Dickinson © pages 57 (right), 63
Gavin Barclay © page 62, 66
Daisy Jellicoe © pages 83, 89, 90 (left), 119
Courtesy of UK Ministry of Defence, UK Crown Copyright: pages 103, 105, 109, 112, 114
PA Images: pages 122, 134, 137
Jade and Karine Kindar-Martin © pages 127, 129